MONEY
SUCCESS
& YOU

Acknowledgements

To Nicole de Montbrun for her editing, patience and suggestions; to Tom Kehoe for his research; to Daryl Woods for designing the cover; and finally to Soraya Othman, my business manager, whose supervision of every detail of this book must be gratefully acknowledged. Thank you.

MONEY
SUCCESS
& YOU

John Kehoe

Published by
Zoetic Inc.
16 Sparkhall Avenue
Toronto, Ontario, Canada M4K 1G5

ISBN 0 9694059 1 X

Produced by Oldstyle Publishing Services
Text design: James Young
Typesetting processed by Everysize Typeart Services
Printed and bound in Australia by Australian Print Group

Contents

It All Starts with You

THIS BOOK is about money and success but, most importantly, it is about you.

Throughout these pages, you will see how financial achievement and self-development can and should go hand in hand with one another. For, indeed, when closely scrutinized, it is evident that the skills needed to become rich and successful are the same skills used to develop character, ability and awareness. Thus, if properly orchestrated our success becomes the means by which we become a greater and more fulfilled human being. And the method by which we can accomplish all this in ourselves is through the art of self-mastery.

Self-mastery is nothing mysterious. It means orchestrating and developing one's capabilities, after looking to see what they might be. It is the ability to know and understand yourself at the deepest level and to make the changes, both internal and external, that are necessary for your growth and success.

Self-mastery operates on the premise that, with training we can grow, and often grow dramatically. That the choices we make in life eventually determine what happens to us. That when we commit ourselves to excel and do whatever is necessary to bring out the best in ourselves, remarkable changes take place.

Participating in our own evolution in this way becomes both rewarding and exhilarating. For, in developing our talents, we will at the same time discover ourselves at an intimate and deeper level. We will awaken what the German writer Goethe called "the genius, power and magic" in ourselves. This is what's so exciting—that we have the ability to do all this. That it is our choice and our choice alone whether we proceed.

This book contains everything you need to know to follow this path. Each chapter contains a principle to be mastered. Some will seem strange and unfamiliar, others will be startlingly simple. Embrace each of them and endeavour to perfect them in your life. For it is in the daily application of these principles where the alchemy takes place. This book is to be lived, not just read. Welcome to the adventure.

Rich Is a Four Letter Word

D O YOU WANT TO BE RICH? It sounds ridiculous. Of course you'd like to be rich, wouldn't everybody? But do you really? Your words might say you do, but your thoughts and actions very often say something entirely different.

Hard to believe? Not really, especially if you understand the workings of the human mind. In fact, you might be shocked to find that there are a number of reasons, playing over and over in your mind, why you don't want to be rich. And what's even more frightening is that you probably don't even know you have these beliefs.

We Are a Product of Our Past Conditioning

What beliefs have you inherited about money? If we grow up in an environment that has limiting beliefs about money, we will inherit those beliefs. If our parents scrimped and saved just to get by, we learn (by example) that money is hard to obtain.

What were you taught as a child? "Don't be greedy"; "Life is full of disappointments"; "Money comes and money goes"; "It's hard to get ahead"—all these thoughts make a lasting impression on a young mind, so that, as adults, we refer to them as reasons why we're not successful. We delude ourselves and will continue to do so until we look closely at our deeply held beliefs and recognize the effects they're having on us.

Every year I conduct a number of seminars worldwide, teaching individuals the principles of money and success. In doing so, I've discovered a very interesting phenomenon: A lot of people are afraid to be rich.

I keep hearing people say such things as: "I'll have to work too hard for it"; "There are more important things than money"; "I don't want to exploit and use people"; "Money will change me in ways I don't like"; and other similar comments.

If you believe that you'll neglect your family, become greedy, lose your friends or have to give up too much to become rich, then no matter how much you want it, there will always be another part of you that will fight it every step of the way.

Even one of these beliefs, deeply ingrained within yourself, is enough to sabotage your efforts in creating wealth. What you need is a set of new beliefs and new models to shape your ideals and inflame your imagination to become rich.

Billionaire Ted Turner is a daring visionary who founded Cable Network News and parlayed a single TV station into an entertainment and communications empire. His brashness and eccentric ways have earned him both respect and condemnation.

But whatever is said about Ted, let it be known that he is also a philanthropist. He sees himself as part of the global solution, a player in making things happen. He believes we can make the world a better place and uses his time and money in many different ways to stimulate change. In 1985, he formed the Better World Society, an organization dedicated to producing socially aware television. Many excellent programmes, which had no chance of funding or commercial appeal, were made as a result. He is a passionate environmentalist as well as an ardent voice against child hunger and he regularly travels the globe meeting business and world leaders in search of solutions. Millions of dollars in grants and donations flow from his wealth to the community every year. He is a visionary; a new, different type of business leader who is making a difference.

Greg Hamilton is a wealthy clothing manufacturer. A multimillionaire, he is well-respected for his business acumen and his commitment to social community projects. Having made a fortune as a successful entrepreneur over the past 20 years, he now conducts a course two nights a week at his local community college on business ethics.

Greg is a loving father, an avid skier and golfer, a successful businessman and an asset to his community. I was privileged to be in his office when Greg signed and handed over a $100,000 cheque to a women's shelter. He had read about its problems in the local paper and decided he wanted to help. It was a powerful experience to watch the faces of those participating and to witness what great achievements can be done when money is put into the right hands. It's a lesson we need to imprint on our consciousness.

Here's the point: until you feel good about having money, and lots of it, you're unlikely to have it. The values and beliefs you have about money will determine how much of it you are eventually going to possess. Convince yourself of the importance of being successful. Recognize that your success can help many people, and your failure will help no one. If you fully understand this, it then becomes your duty and responsibility to succeed. Don't allow yourself to entertain the thought of anything less.

Be inspired by those individuals (and there are many of them) who use money as a vehicle for social change, who make a difference.

Feel good about success, wealth and money. Let no one distort the value and importance of money with their negative views. Hold the vision clear. Money is good. Money is powerful. Money is important. To believe less is to handicap yourself.

Self-Talk

H AVE YOU LISTENED in to what you've been saying to yourself lately? If not, you should be. We talk to ourselves all the time, and what we are saying to ourselves invariably influences our decisions and behaviour.

Each of us has an inner voice which is talking to us all the time. And this inner voice isn't passive. It has very strong opinions on every aspect of your life. It's either helping you and talking you up or it's putting you down. It's filling you with thoughts of fear, worry and confusion, or thoughts of confidence, hope and inspiration. There doesn't seem to be a middle ground. So knowing what it's saying is important.

It's almost as if there was a mental tape recorder playing inside us; and we have tapes for every situation. These tapes consist of beliefs, hopes, worries, fears, desires, opinions and judgements, and we play them over and over within ourselves as different situations arise.

When you mentally repeat to yourself such phrases as "I'll never do it," "I'm always losing," "It'll be another disappointment for me," "Things never go right," you are talking yourself into that exact situation. You begin to expect the worst and actually help it to happen to you.

But the opposite "self-talk" has an empowering effect. Phrases such as "I can do it," "I'm a champion," "I always come through in the end," "I can't lose," "Nothing is going to stop me," reinforce your belief in yourself. It gives you moral support. It's a cheering section inside you. It uplifts and empowers you.

Programming Yourself for Success

I once spent a few days with an artist friend of mine. One morning, upon rising, he announced to me: "Today's the day one hundred things get done." He was behind in a number of his projects and had decided that this was to be an extremely productive day. So, throughout the day he repeated to both himself and me that "Today is the day one hundred things get done." I watched him condition his mind as he busily went from one assignment to another. Some took only a few moments, others a half hour or more, but all the while he kept repeating his affirmation.

Now, I don't know if he actually accomplished a hundred different chores, but by the end of the day, he had accomplished an unbelievable amount and his self-talk assisted him immeasurably.

You can use self-talk in numerous situations. Just find a phrase that represents what you want to have happen to you and begin repeating it over and over to yourself, like a mantra. Do this while driving your car or waiting for an appointment or riding the elevator, and even while you're actually working.

A professional rugby player I know always says to himself whenever he gets the ball, "Nobody can stop me." He repeats it quickly, over and over to himself as he runs and claims it helps a lot. His statistics seem to verify that. Something's working for him, that's for sure.

Sam Butler, a salesman for a financial services firm, who regularly finishes in the top 10% of his company, has the habit of saying to himself before he sees a client, "I'm going to make a great presentation." He takes two minutes to repeat it and makes a better presentation as a result.

Here's an incredible fact (and when you fully grasp the significance of it, it will change forever the way you talk to yourself): You will come to believe whatever you repeat to yourself providing you repeat it often enough. Tell yourself enough times you're a loser and you'll believe it. Tell yourself over and over that you're destined for greatness and that's what you'll accept. And the most exciting part about all this is that you decide what you say. We can't stop the inner tape recorder playing, but we can choose the tapes. Not only can we choose the tapes, but we can actually create them to order.

Be selective with what inner tapes you listen to, and be vigilant. Negative self-talk almost always naturally follows a temporary failure or negative experience. Without even realizing it, on goes the "It's hopeless" tape, or "I'm a loser" tape. Knowing this, we can be on the look-out and catch ourselves quickly, as it happens.

Several days ago I had a visit with my grandfather, who is 103 years old. We talked about encouragement being more constructive than criticism. I love his simple, honest, down-home philosophy and never miss a chance to get him talking about life.

"People respond so well to encouragement," he shared with me, "yet most people continue to use criticism in trying to get people to change or do better. Why don't they use more encouragement?" How true, I thought, and let's remember this when we're dealing with ourselves as well. It's the same principle. Don't be too hard on yourself. Be a good friend. If you want the best from yourself, feed yourself lots of encouragement. Ask yourself, "What can I say to myself today that is supportive and nurturing for me?".

"Just My Luck"

How many times have you heard people use the expression "It's just my luck" to explain away their misfortunes? Have you ever heard someone use it positively? If not, then you've never been out sailing with Jim Burns. Jim is a jewellery wholesaler and a partner in my sailboat. We started using this expression when sailing and, we would inevitably get good weather. "Just our luck," we would chime together, with big grins on our faces as the wind propelled us along. Then, I started using it in other parts of my life. Every time something good happened to me I found myself saying, "Just my luck!" It became like a joke. However, after a few months of doing this, something rather remarkable happened. I actually began thinking of myself as lucky, and as living a charmed life. Without even realizing what I was doing, I became what I was saying to myself—even though it was half in jest. And now I am very lucky, and great, unexpected things continue to happen to me all the time.

I think more than enough has been said to give you the starting point with which to take this technique into your life and begin experimenting with this power. Think of what great and empowering things there are to say to yourself. Don't wait any longer, begin today.

Make People Feel Important

JOHN DEWEY, one of America's most profound philosophers, said that the desire to be important is one of the deepest urges in human nature. William James echoed the same sentiment when he said: "The deepest principle in human nature is the craving to be appreciated." Look around you and see if it isn't so. We all need to be appreciated and acknowledged to know that our contribution makes a difference no matter how small. We need this the same as we need air and water. The person who understands this and who regularly and consistently makes people feel important will not only be surrounded by friends and grateful associates, but will literally write his ticket to wherever he wants to go. It's that important.

I discovered this first-hand working at a summer job between semesters at school. I was a delivery driver for a pharmaceutical company and had about 50 regular customers. One day, I printed up a flyer I had written called "You are a great and marvelous creation". It read "You are special, you are unique, you can do anything" and went on in a short, inspirational message to make people feel good about themselves. With my own money I printed it up and distributed it to all my customers. (Even back then, there was a writer lurking within me.) Little did I realize the effect it would have.

It empowered everyone I gave it to. The smiles on their faces more than compensated for the time and energy I had put into creating it, and many immediately put it up on their walls so they and their customers could see it everyday. But it didn't stop there. Two days later I was called into the personnel manager's office. He was beaming. "What did you do?" he asked. "We're getting all these phone calls thanking us for the pamphlet." He asked to see it and just shook his head in amazement that a delivery driver would take the time and trouble to do such a thing.

A week later, I was brought before the president of the company and introduced as "this is the man who wrote the pamphlet." The president stood up, shook my hand and, in front of my supervisors, praised me lavishly. You'd think I'd discovered insulin the way he was going on. He asked if he could reprint it and distribute it through the other drivers as well. I happily obliged. Suddenly, I was a "star" in the company. Everybody stopped to shake my hand. Salesmen I didn't even know would stop me and say, "You're the one who wrote that pamphlet," and each shared a story about what an impact it had made on them.

I had unwittingly struck a vein of gold, and when I left that job they had a goodbye party for me and everyone, from the president on down, was there. All this for a part-time summer driver who had worked there for only three months. It taught me a valuable lesson I have never forgotten: "Make people feel important and doors will open".

"The dignity and worth of the individual is a very important part of the HP way" says Bill Hewlett, co-founder of the billion-dollar company Hewlett Packard. The HP way? That's what they call it—its people-oriented philosophy has made it one of the most successfully run companies in America. "I believe that men and women want to do a good job", Hewlett continues, "a creative job, and will do so if they are provided with the proper environment to do so. We treat every employee, no matter what position, with respect and we recognize personal achievements wherever we find them." And they go out of their way to find them too!

Their corporate objectives, written in a statement of corporate philosophy, begins with: "The achievements of an organization are the result of the combined efforts of each individual."

Smart companies know and understand this. It's good business to make people feel important. Employees are called "crew members" rather than personnel at McDonald's, "hosts" at Disney Productions and "associates" at J. C. Penney. It makes their people feel important; that they belong; that they are more than just meaningless cogs in a giant wheel. We all need to know this.

Boeing, the most successful aeroplane manufacturer in the world—with last year's sales topping $20 billion (US) knows the wisdom of this philosophy. Every time a new plane is ready, there is a big celebration in which everyone participates. The plane is rolled on to the tarmac and receptionists, secretaries, maintenance men, engineers, vice presidents, all gather together. There are toasts and accolades, and everyone is made to feel that they have contributed to make this happen. And, indeed, they have. But what's important is that Boeing takes the time and effort to reinforce this to them. They want their employees to feel important, needed and appreciated. So they take the time to do it.

Try it yourself. As an experiment, spend one week making everyone you meet feel important. Your clients, customers, fellow workers, wife or husband, the taxi driver— look for opportunities to make people feel special, needed and important. At first, it might seem awkward, but you'll soon get the feel of it and actually start enjoying it. Watch how people respond. Keep it up for one full week and watch what happens both to you and those around you. It will be a startling revelation. It will probably change forever the way you deal with people.

Often when people are made to feel important, talents they never even knew they possessed are unleashed. Stevie Morris is an example. Stevie was a withdrawn, introverted young boy in whom self-confidence was sorely lacking. It certainly didn't help that he was blind as well. However, he overcame his handicap as a result of a single incident that changed his life forever.

One time at school, his teacher called him to help her with a problem. There was a mouse in the classroom, and

21

after many futile attempts to find it, she realized that Stevie had something nobody else possessed: a remarkable pair of ears, which seemed to have developed to compensate for his blindness. She pointed this out to him and encouraged him to use his extraordinary hearing ability. At first, he was shy, but then he reluctantly agreed, and they found the mouse. This was the first time in his life his blindness was an asset. Everyone congratulated and praised him. For the first time in his life, Stevie felt important.

Now, many years later, he says that this act of acknowledgement and appreciation was the beginning of a new life for him. From that point on he became determined to develop his gift of hearing and went on to become one of the greatest singer-songwriters of our time. His name: Stevie Wonder.

Appreciate people. Encourage them. Acknowledge them. Admire them for qualities or talents they possess. Does it mean anything? You bet. "Every man I meet is my superior in some way, in that I learn from him and respect him," said Emerson. Should we do less?

Nothing is more powerful than positive reinforcement. I have never seen a person, however great or exalted his or her station might be, who did not do better work and put forth a greater effort, under the spirit of approval.

How do you make people feel important? Begin by seeing them as important. Start seeing them as a vital part of the whole mechanism. Everyone counts, from your star salesman to the receptionist. Let them know this. With your words, actions, compliments, gifts and cards, there are hundreds of ways to let people know they matter.

Never miss a chance to empower people. Its benefits last far beyond the time it takes to pay a simple compliment and its effects can last for years; even a lifetime. All it takes is a little bit of your time and the awareness that feeling important is a vital need in us all, a need that is largely being unfulfilled. Fill that need and, not only will you feel good, but benefits will flow to you in incredible abundance, and you will be a welcome guest everywhere you go.

Sign the Cheque

IFIRST MET NELSON SKALBANIA, the flamboyant Canadian entrepreneur, during the late 1970s when he was making headlines buying and selling sports franchises, hotels and companies at the rate most other men change their shirts.

It was hard to tell at any given time what he owned, sold, bought, leased or had options on. During a hectic two-year period, he'd made more than $50 million from his activities: not for the faint-hearted, the break-neck speed that he consummated deals. Yet, he taught me a very important lesson that has been invaluable in my business dealings ever since.

"There are only four things that have to be established in every business deal," he said. "First, sign the cheque. Second, sign the cheque. Third, sign the cheque. Fourth, sign the cheque. Everything else is just detail."

There are plenty of people who talk a great game. There are lots of great ideas, plans, proposals, possibilities, probabilities, good intentions, sure things, guarantees, etc., but until the cheque is signed, it's all just so much hot air.

Let me share with you two ways I've used this principle to my great advantage.

First: How to establish if the other party is serious? Ask for a cheque.

Don't be afraid to ask for a cheque. I like to move quickly in my business and I hate it when things are stalled, or going nowhere, because of lack of commitment.

Say I'm involved in a new venture or proposal with other parties. We've had an initial meeting or two and now it's time to move forward. I usually say something like this: "Great idea. I think it has wonderful possibilities. Now, for our next meeting let's get this, this and this done and ... bring a $50,000 (or whatever is appropriate) cheque." BOOM. The bombshell is dropped.

There is nothing like asking for money to be delivered to see where the other party really stands. People talk a big game, and everybody has tremendous ideas and good intentions. But, to me, nothing speaks louder than a signed cheque.

Second: Want to get someone's attention? Write them a cheque.

You're negotiating with another party, it's close and could go either way. At a crucial point in your discussion, take out your chequebook and say, "Look, I'm serious. Let's settle it right now. I'm going to write you a cheque for ... (state the amount)," and begin writing. Don't wait for him to say yes or no, write the cheque, without looking up to see his reaction, and hand it to him. You will feel the electricity in the air.

Dramatic? Yes, and surprisingly effective. It's funny, but very few people are able to resist money when it's offered. It's no longer an abstract profit that might or might not happen, but an actual sum of money in their hands.

This has a powerful psychological impact on people and works an amazing number of times. Nothing, and I repeat, nothing, speaks louder than a signed cheque.

Waking Up in the
Age of Information

W
E ARE LIVING in one of the most exciting periods civilization has ever known—the information age. It is a period of stupendous and radical change. It's frontier land all over again, only with computers, spaceships, lasers and fax machines at our disposal this time around.

The age of information is more than just a catch phrase. It consists of millions upon millions of events that are redefining and shaping the way we work and live.

Charles Darwin's "survival of the fittest" is as appropriate today as it has always been. However, we need to clear up a common misunderstanding of what he meant by "survival of the fittest". He did not mean "fittest" in the sense of the strongest, or most domineering, as is commonly thought. He meant that the best possible fit between organism and environment, is the one that survives and succeeds. The organism that fits best is the one that is most capable of adapting and using its strengths to meet the changes presented to it.

If we are then to be the fittest in today's rapidly changing marketplace, we need to rethink our present situation carefully and begin equipping ourselves with new talents and skills. In the '90s, the fittest will be those who can adapt and change, who can get all the information they need and learn skills quickly, as required.

Knowledge is indeed power and in these times, even more so. A behaviour psychologist at Ford Motor Company said, "The average worker of today will probably have to relearn their job five different times in their career." And he could be underestimating significantly.

You hear it again and again in banks, insurance companies, on the factory floor and in the high-tech think tanks; the echo is loud and clear, "learning new skills is the key that will unlock the door to the opportunities of the future."

"The future of work," wrote Canadian philosopher and futurist Marshall McLuhan, "now consists of learning a living rather than earning a living". In this light, survival of the fittest takes on a whole new meaning.

If indeed this is the case, and all the indicators point in this direction, then the most important question you can ever ask yourself, and you should ask it of yourself today, is, "What do I need to learn?" If you do, and act intelligently on the information you receive, you will be well-positioned for the enormous array of opportunities that these changes are bringing. Not only will you survive, but you will succeed in a big way.

The Marketplace in the '90s

TWENTY THOUSAND million dollars (US) changes hands every day in North America (United States and Canada combined).* $20,000 million changed hands yesterday. $20,000 million is changing hands today and another $20,000 million or so will change hands tomorrow. It's happening every day, 365 days a year, and the amounts are not dwindling, they're growing. You should be taking your fair share of all this money in action. If not, you're missing out on a golden opportunity.

Isn't it fabulous and exciting to be living among such wealth? We don't fully realize the immense opportunities available to those of us who live in a free market economy that allows every individual equal opportunity to earn as much money as he or she is able.

The marketplace is no respecter of age, race, colour or sex. It rewards ingenuity and service wherever it is found. The greater the ingenuity and service, the greater the reward. If you have a good idea, product or service, market it effectively and follow the principles of success, you too will reap the rewards. The dynamics of the marketplace

*United Nations Economics Statistics, United Nations Publishing, Geneva, 1987.

guarantees it. Anyone telling you differently is ill-informed. The marketplace rewards abundantly and lavishly to those who understand this and fulfill the necessary requirements. "Find a need and fill it" has been the maxim in the marketplace for thousands of years and is still the rule today. The market is waiting.

Recession or Boom—The Marketplace is Loaded

I laugh when people talk about how there's no money out there during a recession. Are they kidding? Do they live on the moon? No money? Why, the marketplace is loaded.

Boom times and recessionary times are statistical terms used by economists to describe the enormous flow of capital and growth in this wealthy nation of ours. Don't get spooked by the terms.

Let me use an analogy to give a simplified explanation of what is happening during a recession. A powerful locomotive is barrelling down the tracks at 100 miles an hour. Nothing can stop it. It is being fuelled by its own energy. Then, it slows to 90 miles an hour for a while before it picks up full steam again. Slowing the train to 90 miles an hour isn't going to derail it. There's no cause to panic. It's still a powerful locomotive travelling at an incredibly high speed. It's still a force to be reckoned with. The same with our economy. Any economy as diverse and abundant as ours that has a slight slow-down and operates at 90% efficiency is still pumping incredible amounts of money into the system. There's money and opportunity

out there. Don't be fooled or lulled into believing anything different. Learn to see it in its proper perspective
and take full advantage of the present situation. Let others
panic if they want to.

Get a Grasp of How a Marketplace Works

Imagine yourself transported back hundreds of years to a
small village in the English countryside. It's the era of
Robin Hood, King Richard III and the Holy Crusades.
And, today is market day. You find yourself strolling
through the market, which is a hive of activity. Wares of
every description are available. Goods and services are
being sold for a profit. There is a blacksmith catering to
the needs of the merchants who cart their wares by horse.
He employs two helpers and is considering hiring a third.
There are merchants selling silk, herbs, pots and pans,
bows and arrows, clothes, tools, household necessities.
Farmers are displaying their produce, each priced for a
quick sale. There is a small pub and a place to eat and
relax. A musician is playing tunes on his mandolin for donations. He is approached by a man whose daughter is
getting married. How much would he charge? A story
teller has a small crowd on the edge of their seats as he
mesmerizes them with tales of the feats of fabled heroes.
A promoter is putting up posters announcing an archery
contest to be held soon. A cash prize to the winner, entry
just two pence. He hopes to make a profit. It is the free
enterprise system. Capitalism in motion.

Some merchants are doing exceedingly well, others are
just barely getting by and still others are losing money

and will soon disappear. It is colourful and exciting and everyone is plying their trade to the best of their ability. This is how the marketplace works and it's easily understood on a small scale.

Now magnify this small marketplace by ten million times or so. Add hundreds of thousands of variables, and so many unaccounted for circumstances, that you can't even begin to fathom its size and complexity. This is a rough approximation of our marketplace today. It is so rich, diverse and unknowable that it defies description. People are making fortunes in literally thousands of occupations and fields, many you haven't even heard of let alone thought of entering. Opportunities are everywhere. Money is everywhere. The marketplace is bursting at its seams with money, opportunities and possibilities and they aren't going away but growing by leaps and bounds.

Get the spirit of it all. Imagine the possibilities and potential. Picture in your mind how much money there is in circulation. There's $20,000 million changing hands even while you read this book. Go ahead and get your fair share.

Find Your Passion

A RECENT NATIONAL POLL revealed that more than 80% of North America's working population do not enjoy the work they do. This is a profoundly tragic statistic, considering that work consumes so much of our lives. Nor is it a good formula for success because when you study closely people who are successful (as I have over the years), it becomes abundantly clear that their achievements are directly related to the enjoyment they derive from their work. This really struck home to me while I was writing this book. Since this is a book about money and success, I decided to send each of my successful friends a copy of the manuscript so I could get their feedback. As I finished my list and was reading over the names, I suddenly realized that every single one of them had made their fortunes in areas they enjoyed working in. One was in publishing, another was a clothes designer, one in law, still another in home renovating—and so it went. They had found their passion, devoted themselves to it and had prospered. Every single one of them was doing what they loved doing.

It got me thinking: Has anybody ever made a fortune doing what they dislike? I thought about it for a while and you know what? I couldn't think of anyone. Not one. Something to seriously ponder if you presently find yourself trying to get ahead working at a job or occupation you dislike.

Do What You Love, the Money Will Follow

Lars-Eric Lindblad loved travelling. As he backpacked his way to some of the more exotic locations around the world, he thought of what he would do when he eventually returned home. Nothing seemed appealing; and then, he suddenly had an idea. "There are probably others like myself," he thought " who wants to experience a more adventurous type of travel. Why not start a business to cater to their specific needs?" So that's what he did. He started his own travel agency, Lindblad Travel, offering adventurous trips to offbeat locations—the Gobi Desert, Antarctica, the Galapagos Islands. The people in the travel industry told him he was sure to fail. "You can't make money offering just adventure packages." Nobody thought he could succeed, but succeed he did, and in a very big way. And 200,000 customers later, his travel business is booming. Here's the lesson for those of you who wish to follow your dream; the real key to Lindblad's success is that he chose something that he was excited about, something he believed in, and from the beginning, he did the thousand and one things that had to be done to make it a success.

Peter Moore hated his job as a bank manager. Although he liked dealing with people, he felt stuck in his choice of occupations and felt he wasn't using his talents to the maximum. He wanted more. Realizing that his people skills would be well-suited to sales, he began thinking of a career in selling. But selling what? Then, one day as he was handling the affairs of a woman whose husband had recently died, it hit him. Why not sell life insurance?

Peter's experience as a bank manager had given him experience dealing with families who are left without proper financial support. He believed absolutely in the service and excitedly began researching all the available companies to see which ones had the best policies. When he had made his decision, he approached the sales manager and told him what he'd done and why he wanted to sell life-insurance for them. He was given a job on the spot.

Within one year, he became one of their top salesmen and eventually became the district sales manager for the entire West Coast. He succeeded because he found something he could do with conviction. Something that felt right. He found his passion.

Stephen Sandler thought his grandmother's mustard was the best in the world. Nothing else he had ever tasted even came close. Everyone else who tasted it at his house said the same. Then, one day, he had a wild idea. "Why not bottle it and sell it?" But then came the doubts. There are already lots of brands of mustard available. I have no real business experience. There's stiff competition for shelf space. Why would they give an unknown a chance?" And there were hundreds of other reasons why not to do it. But he really believed his grandmother's mustard was better than anything else available and this thought kept nagging at him. So, he decided to give it a try.

He made twelve jars, had some labels printed and went to visit the local delicatessens. He told them he already had a company that produced the mustard and offered them a free jar as a sample. Much to his surprise, he received an order for 120 jars from one of them.

"At six jars an hour," he laughed, "I didn't think I'd ever get through that first order." He started by making it in his own kitchen and it eventually took over the house before he had to move to larger premises. Sandler Mustard is now sold in delicatessens all across the country and his small company, just barely out of infancy, is now worth over $2 million. Stephen Sandler found his passion—and it was mustard.

"People whose whole objective is making money, usually don't," says Jerry White, professor of entrepreneurial studies at the University of Toronto, Canada. He should know. He's made it his business to study successful entrepreneurs and to teach others their winning ways, and the one message that came through loud and clear was: Find a product or service you can believe in passionately because without this, you will not succeed.

What is your calling? In what areas are you best suited? How can you find a livelihood that will nourish and fulfill you?

You start by simply believing in yourself. Take stock of your assets, your strong points and see how you can best use them. Very often it's a lack of self-confidence that keeps us in positions we don't like. If this is the case then embark upon a daily program designed to build self-confidence. Make it your first priority and once this is achieved, your perspectives too will have changed. Options that didn't exist before will suddenly make themselves known. Things look different when you're standing on a mountain rather than wandering in the valley. Self-confidence puts you on that mountain.

Remind yourself that you possess a powerful subconscious mind that will guide you. Go to it daily and let it supply you with the answers you are looking for. Drink deeply from this inner source.

You might discover, upon close examination, that new skills and talents are required before you can successfully follow your chosen calling. If so, you're in luck. Each of us has the ability to train ourselves and become proficient in any area we choose. You can do and become whatever you want. To believe less is to sell yourself short.

"Every calling is great when greatly pursued," said Oliver Wendell Holmes. Whether you're selling life insurance, designing buildings, managing a company, writing a book, marketing new products, cutting hair—find the passion and excitement in it. If you can, you will succeed like you never have before. Follow your dream. Trust your instincts. Find that something that you can believe in passionately and give it your all. Do what you love; the money will follow.

Learn to Love the
Word "No"

THERE IS A FAMOUS LINE in Francis Ford Coppola's *Apocalypse Now,* the classic film that is a brilliant depiction of the Vietnam war. A commanding officer, portrayed by Robert Duvall, is standing in the jungle, naked to the waist. It's morning and already steaming hot. "I love the smell of napalm in the morning," he announces, taking in a long, drawn out-breath, "it smells like victory!"

Well, I feel the same way about the word "no". I love the sound of the word "no". To me, it means action; something is happening. "No's" have a way of eventually leading to the word "yes".

Almost everyone hates the the word "no". Salespeople, entrepreneurs, children, lovers, inventors, visionaries all hate the word "no".

Yet, it's an indisputable fact of business that if you're not hearing the word "no", you're probably not hearing the word "yes" either. Business involves hearing a whole lot more "no's" than "yes's". There are very few organizations that don't operate on this principle. It's obvious. The more "no's" you hear, the more "yes's" are bound to happen.

In sales, if you hear a thousand "no's" you'll probably hear a hundred "yes's", maybe even two or three hundred. But if you aren't hearing "no's", then you are probably not hearing any "yes's" either.

People avoid making sales calls or contacts or phone calls because they're afraid of the word "no". *What if the person says "no",* they think. When you hear the word "no", remember there is a "yes" just around the corner. When you hear your second "no", the yes is even closer. And the third is closer still. Love the word "no", it's the sound of success in motion. When you're not hearing it, you're in deep trouble.

The Cy Young Award is given each year to the best pitcher in both the American and National Leagues. It is a most coveted award. Its winners are a who's who of baseball: Sandy Kovak, Brett Saberhagen, Nolan Ryan. The list goes on and on.

However, few people realize that this award is named after the man who holds baseball's record for most career defeats. Yes, that's defeats, not victories. Cy Young lost 313 games, more than any major league pitcher in the history of baseball. Why would they name an award after someone who holds the record for the most defeats, you might ask? Wouldn't it be more appropriate to name it after the person who had the most victories? Well, they did. It's the same man.

Did you know that the great home-run king, Babe Ruth, held the record for the most strike-outs of any major league player during his career?

A friend of mine, who sells life insurance and is consistently the top salesman for his company, once told me, "I probably hear the word 'no' twice or three times as much as my co-workers."

Nobody counts the "no's". Nobody cares about the defeats. The only thing that counts are the victories, the successes—that's what matters.

The next time you feel dejected because someone says "no", remember "no" is just the way that leads you to the "yes's".

Goals Are Crucial

I LOVE SAILING. I have a beautiful 32-foot wooden sloop hand-built by a friend of mine who is a master West Coast craftsman. I go out in it as much as possible. Sometimes, I'll take the boat out in the afternoon and just sail around the harbour, back and forth, enjoying the sun and wind in my face. I don't end up going anywhere, but that's because I'm sailing just for the sake of sailing.

Other times I'll take off for a week or more. Occasionally, even for a month or two. At these times, I have clearly defined destinations. Each day, I study the charts carefully before I begin and set myself a course for the day. I navigate. Choose and trim the sails according to wind conditions, correct my course and make changes as necessary. I watch for and recognize signs along the way; a reef here, an island there, at each point of the journey I try to establish both where I am and where I'm going. I can't imagine doing it any other way. It can't be done any other way. Imagine sailing off with no charts or no course, just with hope and determination that you would arrive? How ridiculous and yet that's what we do when we head off in life, hoping and wanting the best but setting no goals on how to achieve it. Is it any wonder we don't arrive?

"The reason most people don't achieve their goals in life," remarked author and lecturer Dennis Waitley, rather dryly, "is because they didn't have any in the first place." Everyone wants to be healthy, happy, successful and hundreds of other things, but not everyone has goals that map out how they will achieve these objectives.

Are You Like Alice in Wonderland?

For those of you who have not read Lewis Carrol's classic *Through the Looking Glass* since childhood, I suggest you read it again because it is written for adults, just as surely as for children, and is still very entertaining.

One scene has Alice completely and thoroughly lost, not knowing which way to turn, so she asks the Cheshire cat, perched rather precariously on a tree limb, for some help.

"Would you tell me, please which way I ought to go from here?" asks Alice.

"That depends a good deal on where you want to go," replies the cat.

"I don't much care where," says Alice.

"Then it doesn't much matter which way you go," came the reply.

"So long as I get somewhere," Alice adds as an explanation.

"Oh, you're sure to do that," grinned the cat.

I love that. It's so real and absurd and yet all too familiar in the way we often live our lives. We make a tragic error when we mistake working hard and being busy with having goals. We assume that if we're working hard we must be getting ahead. But working hard and being busy trying to get ahead without specific, clearly defined goals on how to do it, is living in a fool's paradise. And the sooner we recognize this, the better.

What Do You Want Out of Life?

What do you want out of life? Do you know? If you're not sure it's probably time for some serious, self-reflection. Each of us has certain times in our life when we need to stop and take stock of where we are and where we are going.

If you feel this is one of those times for you, let me give you some suggestions on how to go about it.

Set aside one hour a day for at least a month, in which you reflect upon your life. Give yourself some time. Don't rush it. Each day, make a list of the five most important things you want to achieve in your life. Do this every day. The reason I say every day is that your list will change from day to day. Some items will seem important one day and not the next. Others will be repeated over and over.

Here's a little trick that could also help you. Imagine you're 80 years old, looking back at your life. What would you like to have seen happen? What would you regret most not doing? This can help you get a clear picture of what you really want to do.

The goals you set for yourself will inevitably determine the circumstances and situations you will meet in life. This being so, choose wisely and pursue those things that are closest to your heart. There is no point in having goals that you think you probably should achieve, when deep down you don't really want them at all.

A poet once wrote:

> One ship sails east, another west
> by the selfsame winds that blow.
> 'Tis the set of the sail and not the gale,
> that determines the way they go.

Tips on Achieving Your Goals

1. Have some.

2. Write down on a piece of paper what it is you want to achieve. Unless it is written down and regularly focused on, you are almost certain not to achieve it. You must never lose sight of why you are doing the thousands of little details needed to achieve it.

3. Break the larger goals into smaller goals. This means having short-term and intermediate objectives as well as the overall end result.

4. Be specific about what you want. It's not enough to say I want to be wealthy, healthy, happy and successful. These goals are too vague and undefined. You want to be wealthy? What's wealthy? How much money do you

want to have? How much do you want to make this year? The next five years? How are you going to do it? You want to be healthy? Be more specific. Do you want to lose weight? How much? Do you want to tone up? What are you going to do—join a gym, go swimming? How often? Set goals and be specific.

5. Begin to plot a step-by-step process that will take you to your final objective. Some steps will almost certainly be missing in the beginning but chart yourself a course anyway, and, most importantly, begin immediately to put your plan into action.

6. Establish a time limit on when you are to achieve your goal. There's an old saying that a task will always expand to fill the amount of time you give to it, and it's true. Expect of yourself results within a specific time.

7. Master all the principles of this book, giving special attention to Mental Rehearsal and Harnessing Your Subconscious Mind. I suggest you read these chapters over once every day until you become totally convinced of the power they contain to help you achieve your goals.

Mental Rehearsal

WHAT IS THE ONE FACTOR above all others that distinguishes those who succeed from those who fail?

"It's all in the mind," says movie star and body builder Arnold Schwarzenegger. A multi-millionaire, successful real estate tycoon, movie star, body builder, five-time winner of Mr. Universe, Arnold has it made. But it wasn't always so. Arnold can remember back when he had nothing except a belief that his mind was the key to getting where he wanted to go.

"When I was very young, I visualized myself being and having what it was I wanted. Mentally, I never had any doubts about it. The mind is really so incredible. Before I won my first Mr Universe, I walked around the tournament like I owned it. The title was already mine. I had won it so many times in my mind that there was no doubt I would win it.

"Then, when I moved on to the movies, the same thing. I visualized myself being a successful actor and earning big money. I could feel and taste the success. I just knew it would all happen."

Chris Pollein was a member of the world-renowned, West German freestyle ski team that won the European Cup six times between 1976 and 1982.

"Part of our training programme involved working with a psychologist to increase the power of our minds. After training on the slopes, we were placed in a state of meditation and encouraged to totally repeat the slope runs in our minds, visualizing each bump and movement of the routine. We worked as hard training mentally as we did physically. Excellence in athletics as well as in business depends primarily on having a clear mental picture of that activity."

Chris should know, she not only has her six medals, but she now has her own successful consulting firm teaching business and sports groups how they, too, can benefit from the same techniques.

Bryan Edwards, one of Australia's top life-insurance salesmen, a man of infectious good humour and spirits, spends 10 minutes every evening before he goes to bed running over in his mind his next day's calls. He pictures himself making his presentation to each client. He sees them being receptive and gladly taking out a policy with him. He imagines a very productive day with lots of sales. He does this for 10 minutes before he goes to bed and 10 minutes on rising in the morning—a total of 20 minutes each day. Bryan Edwards sells life insurance with the ease and skill that most other salesman only dream about.

Three different people with totally different goals and objectives in life, yet all are using the same technique to create and influence their reality—the technique of mental rehearsal.

Here's How It's Done

Fix in your mind what it is you want to achieve. Then, imagine yourself having it. Let your mind linger on the thoughts of making the perfect presentation, winning the big contract, getting the job you want, or whatever it is you desire. Run it over and over in your mind like an inner movie. Don't concern yourself that it's only a mental image: Lose yourself completely in the images you are creating and become those images, living it as if it is happening to you now, this very moment. Feel the emotions, the excitement, the sense of accomplishment.

Spend five to ten minutes daily on this exercise. The more times you do it, the more potent the image becomes and the greater its effect. Practise until a clear mental picture of the desired outcome is imprinted in your mind. Then, when you think of possibilities that could happen to you, these are the images that will first come to mind and they will come clearly and powerfully. Practising and mentally rehearsing what you want to have happen to you is not just idle daydreaming. You are creating powerful images within you that the mind calls upon and uses.

Any thought put into your mind, and nourished regularly, will produce results in your life.

Let me share with you a University of Illinois experiment. Student basketball players were divided into three groups, tested for their ability to score baskets, and each group's results were recorded. The first group was then directed to come into the gym every day for a month to practise shooting, the second group was told to engage in no practise at all, and the third group was told to engage in a very different sort of practise. They didn't step foot in the gym, but instead, stayed in their dorms mentally imagining themselves there practising. For half an hour each day they "saw" themselves throwing the ball and scoring baskets and improving dramatically. They continued this inner "practise" every day. After a month, the three groups were tested again.

The first group (those who practised shooting everyday) showed a 26% improvement in their scores. The second group (those who didn't practise) showed no improvement. And the third group—who, remember, had practised only in their minds—improved equally as much as the group that had practised for real.

This world of ours is not a pile of brick and stone. It is a living, dynamic system of energy. Every thought you have impresses itself upon this system and its effect is felt. You are creating your reality through what you are thinking.
Thought is forever attempting to find form, looking for an outlet, trying to manifest itself. It is the nature of thought to try and materialize into its physical equivalent. Although a single, unaided thought hasn't much power, just repeat this particular thought over and over again. Through repetition, the thought becomes concentrated and directed and its force magnified many times. The more it is repeated, the more energy and power it generates and the more readily it is able to manifest.

The technique of mental rehearsal and other mind power techniques are easy to learn and simple to practise. I know because, in addition to using it myself with great success, I've personally taught thousands of others and have seen, first-hand, the results they've achieved.

Begin using this technique today, in any area of your life you wish to see improvement, and within weeks you will be amazed at the results.

Luck

"I am a great believer in luck and I find the harder I work, the more I have of it."

Stephen Leacock, Canadian humourist

"Luck is when opportunity meets preparation."

A. J. Foyt, four-time winner, Indianopolis 500

THESE ARE TWO QUOTATIONS about luck that pretty well sum up my opinion on the matter.

Nobody gets rich because of luck, unless they win the lottery, and the odds against that are about 10 million to one, depending on the lottery.

Riches come because of principles that are applied persistently. Yet, you continue to hear people say how lucky he or she was to was to land that big contract. Luck? I don't think so.

Opportunities Are Everywhere

OPPORTUNITIES ARE EVERYWHERE, you just have to open your eyes. But not your ordinary eyes. Your opportunity eyes. Ones that are trained to look for and identify opportunities wherever they may be. To do this you must understand that opportunities are rarely announced by neon signs that flash: "Opportunity. Opportunity. Here I am." It would be great if they did. More likely they are disguised as problems or difficulties, or inconsequential events. Opportunities are everywhere, but we don't see them because we haven't attuned ourselves to them.

One of the largest diamonds in the world was found by a nine-year-old South African girl. It was the size of a small fist and was found beside a walkway that was passed by hundreds of people every day. However, there was something about that rock that made this little girl pick it up and take it to her father, who, having worked in the mines, suspected it might be more than just a "pretty rock." His suspicion was right, and after it was cut and polished, it was worth more than $2 million.

Chances are, you too wouldn't recognize a raw diamond if you saw one. A diamond in its natural state looks much different than when it's cut and polished and ready for mounting on a ring or pendant.

Let me share with you an incident that happened several years ago on Easter morning. I hid some presents all around my business manager's living room while she was sleeping. I then woke her and said I thought the Easter Bunny had arrived and hidden some presents. She was thrilled and began looking for them. After about 15 minutes, she found three and thanked me profusely. "There's more than that," I said, which immediately had her searching again for more. She found a couple more and we then sat down to breakfast. While we were eating, I casually mentioned, "Too bad you didn't find the good ones," with a mischievous look in my eye.

"There's more?" She asked incredulously.

"There are ten." I announced. That's all she needed to hear and, ignoring breakfast, she methodically began going over the same area, but this time searching everywhere, looking in every nook and cranny. Nothing was overlooked, and finally she found all of them. It was lots of fun, and we laughed about it for months. We still laugh about it today when we think back on that incident, but there's an important lesson here to learn.

When I initially told her I had hidden some presents, she looked everywhere and finding three, stopped. When I informed her there were more she looked again and finding two more stopped again, although she had found only half the presents. It was only when I told her there were 10 presents altogether that she methodically searched and searched until she found them all. Had I said nothing, she would have settled for the original three she'd found.

What are you settling for in your life? What are you being told? What do you believe? If you believe there are no opportunities or very few opportunities left, chances are you won't find any. But if you believe that the times we live in are, literally, bursting with opportunities, you'll look till you find them.

An associate of mine had the good fortune of being seated at the same table as the late oil billionaire John Paul Getty at a charity fund-raising event. A young man also at the table was lamenting the fact that all the good opportunities had been taken. There was no place for the big killing anymore. If only he'd been born 30 years earlier.

John Paul listened patiently and then felt the need to answer the young man. His words bear careful consideration. "Never has there been greater opportunities for success then there are today," spoke the great man. "The rapid growth of technology and the diversity of products and services now available will open up opportunities we can't even imagine today. There has never been a more exciting time to make money than today. Times of great change bring great opportunities, and these are times of great change." John Paul Getty died in 1978. Imagine if he could see what's happening today. If he thought things were changing rapidly in the late 1970s, imagine what he would say about today's rapidly changing business environment.

All ages have lamented about the missed opportunities. There were people a hundred years ago who said all the good opportunities were gone. They said the same in the 1920s, the '30s, the '40s, the '50s. It's laughable of course but each generation seems to feel that all the good opportunities have come and gone. What do you think they'll say about the 1990s, twenty or thirty years from now? No opportunities? Who are you kidding?

One final word about opportunities before I leave the subject (and I hope this will put to rest the myth of no opportunities once and for all). Every time you find yourself thinking there are no opportunities around, remind yourself of this indisputable fact: There are people who haven't been born yet who will one day make fortunes, who will climb to the top of the very industry you now find yourself employed, who will start new businesses that will prosper, and pioneer new industries that in turn will spawn even more opportunities.

There will be great men and women who will be the leaders and champions in business, sports and the arts. So, if they are going to do it, and they aren't even born yet, what about you? What's your excuse? Don't you, in fact, have a head start on them?

Develop the eyes and instincts that recognize opportunities wherever they are, and you'll be pleased at what you find.

Developing a Pleasing Personality

PEOPLE WOULD RATHER DO BUSINESS with people they like than those they don't. This is so obvious that it hardly needs stating, yet so many of us, when dealing with people, go through the motions as if they were mechanical acts.

You might be able to separate yourself from your product or service but almost everyone else you come in contact with cannot. From another's perspective, you and your product are a package. Like it or not, who you are is either an asset or a liability to your success.

This being said, doesn't it make sense to develop a personality that is pleasing and attractive to other people? Oh … I can hear the howls of protest already: "This is who I am"; "People can either accept me or not"; "I can't change"; "I'm not going to be somebody I'm not."

What nonsense. Lighten up. Why not make some changes? Your personality is a creation. You can change any part you don't like. Take Benjamin Franklin as an example.

Franklin, one of the founding fathers of the American Confederation, was a man with a brilliant mind. Nobody who had any contact with him doubted this. However, he felt his personality could be worked on so he resolved to make some changes and, in his autobiography, he shares the methods by which he achieved this.

He made a list of 13 qualities he wished to adopt. Having made a thorough self-examination, he knew what he needed to develop in himself. "I made a little book, in which I allotted a page for each of the virtues. Then I charted my progress, as it was my intention to acquire the habit of all these virtues."

Realizing he could not attempt to acquire them all at once, he picked one a week and concentrated on living that quality for the full week. The next week he went on to the second quality, until he had done all 13. Then he began again. He was able to complete this cycle four times in a year. This practise was so successful that his friends and associates were amazed with the changes.

Benjamin Franklin went on to become one of the most in-fluential men of his time. A creative inventor and brilliant statesman, he was respected and admired by his peers. Would he have accomplished all this without having worked on his personality? We will never know, but I somehow doubt it.

Your personality is either drawing or repelling people. When you fully realize this, you will understand the importance of creating a personality that attracts people and opportunities to you.

A recent study showed that the 10 most admired qualities in a person are:

1. Sense of humour
2. Sincerity
3. Honesty
4. Openness and receptiveness
5. Positive attitude
6. Compassion
7. Patience
8. Good listening ability
9. Confidence
10. Politeness

How many of these qualities do you possess? Test yourself. Or better yet, ask someone who is close to you and knows you well to do an evaluation. Ask for honesty and brace yourself for the result. It's often a sobering realization to find out we're not as perfect as we like to think.

If you have all 10, you're operating at 100% efficiency on the personable scale. But very few people will be at that level. If you find that you have five of these qualities or less, then there's work to be done. Let's assume for a moment that you have five. If you add one more quality, you've improved by 20%. Add two qualities and you've increased by 40%. That's incredible growth. Anybody doing so is sure to notice startling changes in their life.

As a child, how you were raised, what you experienced, were often dictated by circumstances—and by others. But, as an adult, your personality and character are under your control and entirely your own responsibility, you can hold no other person responsible for who you are. If there are parts of you that you don't like, why accept them? Resolve to change. If there are qualities you admire in others, make them yours.

Your personality is an evolution of your thoughts and habits. As your thoughts and habits change, so does your personality. How you act today and tomorrow will determine what you will become.

It's an exhilarating feeling to realize that it's not a matter of discovering who we are so much as deciding what we want to be, and then becoming it. Don't be afraid to change.

Desire

KNOWING WHAT ONE WANTS is not enough. Wishing or hoping is of little value. It is desire that gives you the needed momentum and inspiration. Fuel your desire daily and watch the small spark of hope, that now exists within you, ignite into a blazing fire of determination. Nothing else is more important and crucial to your success.

All the great men and women achievers of the past have had (amongst them) one, overwhelming similarity—a burning desire to achieve their objectives.

Thomas Edison experienced more than 10,000 failures before he perfected the light bulb. His desire to succeed never waned.

Wilbur and Orville Wright suffered humiliation and ridicule for years for daring to believe they could make a vehicle fly in the air. Yet it was the strength of their purpose and desire that led them to produce the first successful aeroplane.

Ted Turner knew he wanted a media and communications empire, so with the aid of a satellite, he beamed the programming that came out of his small Atlanta television station across America. He founded Cable Network News, his flagship operation, which, despite his best efforts, lost $77 million in its first five years. But Ted never wavered.

During this time, he had a sign on his desk that read "Lead, follow or get out of the way". He knew what he wanted and where he was going, and nothing was going to stop him. His burning desire overcame all else. Today, his media empire is a resounding international success, worth billions of dollars.

A strong, burning desire to obtain and possess the goal you are pursuing is the starting point of all achievement.

This isn't a vague wish or a simple hope, it is something much more powerful. Burning desire, when properly ignited, takes on a life and power of it's own and empowers you in hundreds of different ways.

There is an old parable of a Zen monk and his student walking by the river. When the young student begins to plead with his master, "How do I become enlightened? What must I do?" the master grabs him roughly, pulls him into the river and pushes him under the water so he is completely submerged.

The Zen master continues to hold the student under water and, after a minute, the student begins thrashing frantically. But still the master holds his hand under the water. Desperately the student tries to free himself, but to no avail. Finally, just at the point of drowning, the master releases his grip and the student surfaces, gasping for air.

"What were you thinking while I held you under the water?" the master asked. "At first I thought of many things," the student answered. "But after a few seconds, when there was no sign that you would let me up, all I could think of was: Air! Air! Air! Give me air!"

"When you desire enlightenment with the same intensity," said the master smiling, "you will soon have it."

The same applies to achieving your goals. Hoping, wishing, wanting, needing do not count. You must desire it with your whole being. Desire is the fuel that propels you towards your objectives and influences your thoughts and actions.

I don't mean that you should become obsessive, thinking about it every moment of every day until nothing else matters. But, would you be willing to spend 10 minutes a day? How about five minutes in the morning and five in the evening, thinking about your goals, inflaming your desires to the point where it takes on a life and power of it's own?

Follow this three-point plan and watch it work wonders for you:

Step 1: Write down a clear, concise statement of what it is you wish to obtain.

Step 2: Outline what you intend to do to achieve this objective. There is no such thing as something for nothing. What skills, knowledge, disciplines and actions will you obtain or practise? Be clear and concise.

Step 3: Promise to yourself to let nothing stop you from obtaining your objectives. Make a commitment to yourself to do whatever is necessary to achieve your goal. Be firm in your resolution.

Read this statement over, twice every day. Once, upon rising in the morning, and once again before you go to sleep and begin immediately to put this plan to work. When reading your statement, magnetize your mind to the reality of achieving your goal. See and feel yourself already in possession of that which you desire. As days turn into weeks, and then months, this ritual will be the source of a great amount of power and inspiration for you.

Strong desire acts as a magnet attracting the people, circumstances and situations needed to achieve your goal. No other method can replace it. It is indispensable to your success.

Remember, first you fuel the desire, then the desire fuels you. This is such an important principle to understand that I will repeat it again.

First you must fuel the desire, then the desire will fuel you.

Are Your Goals Large Enough?

D R ROBERT SCHULLER, the well known inspirational evangelist, once stated that it was harder for him to raise $1200 for a new dishwasher than it was to raise $1,000,000 for a "tower of hope". This doesn't make logical sense except when you realize big goals stimulate and inspire people to action. Big goals get the adrenalin flowing and have a way of making things happen. Big goals are powerful.

But isn't there a danger (some say) in picking a goal that's too big, too large? In answer to this, let me say quite emphatically, yes. But there is as much a danger in having a goal that is too small. Because, if it's not large enough to inspire you, to stimulate you, to inflame your imagination, chances are you won't achieve it, and this is a fact.

Patanjali, the founder of yoga in ancient India, put it this way: "When you are inspired by some great purpose, some extraordinary project, all your thoughts break their bonds. Your mind transcends limitations, your consciousness expands in every direction, and you find yourself in a new, great and wonderful world. Dormant forces, faculties and talents become alive and you discover yourself to be a greater person by far than you ever dreamed yourself to be."

I discovered this first-hand as I was about to embark on my first lecture tour of Australia in 1981. I was in Thailand vacationing with the Australian promoter. We had made an arrangement that she was to receive 20% of the profits for her work. I casually mentioned that I thought she would be making about $7500 a month plus expenses. I thought she'd be very pleased. You can imagine my surprise when she said that wasn't good enough and what she needed to take was $15,000 a month, and that's what she was counting on.

I didn't know what to say. I knew the reality of the situation and what we'd probably be earning. I'd been in the business for five years and for her to earn $15,000 a month, I would have to make more than double what I'd ever done previously. I knew that was impossible.

I wrestled with this for several days. What were my options? I could pay her more and take a smaller percentage myself, or she could settle for $7500. After all, it was a considerable wage. Nothing felt right until I realized that maybe, just maybe, it was possible to make more money in Australia than I had anticipated.

I will forever remember the exact moment that this thought came into my mind because it marks a turning point in my life. I was walking along the beach, while the sun was setting, when I thought, why not make twice as much money? It would solve the problem perfectly. At first, I thought it was impossible, but something within me said it was possible. As the thought of earning twice as much money became a possibility in my mind, I became charged in a way I'd never experienced before. I felt more powerful than the setting sun. I was alive and transformed in a whole new way.

Over the next two weeks, as I walked along the beaches, new ideas, new ways of marketing myself, new plans kept flooding into my mind. What had been totally impossible two weeks ago was now not only possible, but even probable—if I followed my plan. I couldn't believe the change.

We arrived in Australia and I had the most successful lecture tour of my career. The promoter got her $15,000 a month for the duration of the tour and I earned more money than I'd ever done in my life.

However, I received something even more valuable than the money. I learned that opportunities open up when you open up your thoughts. I knew then that the only change one has to make is within oneself to achieve any goal. Don't waste your time asking yourself "How am I going to do it? How will it happen?" Just make the decision to do it and then watch the ideas and plans follow. Large goals have a momentum and power that give you the means to achieve them, if you will only set yourself to the task. Incredible as it seems, it often takes no more effort to achieve a large goal than it does a small goal. This universal truth is accurately summed up in the following poem:

I bargained with life for a penny
And life would pay no more,
However, I begged at evening
When I counted my scanty store.

For life is a just employer
He gives you what you ask,
But once you have set the wages,
Why, you must bear the task.

I worked for a menial's hire
Only to learn dismayed,
That any wage I had asked of life
Life would have willingly paid.

Remember this as you make your decisions on what it is you want from life.

If You Don't Know—Ask!

EVER NEED MORE INFORMATION about a project, a service or a market, and don't know where to get it?

Why not pick up the phone and ask someone who might know? You can call a total stranger. And it's unbelievably effective in getting the information you need.

I first watched this technique in action while sitting in the luxurious office of a successful real estate developer. He was contemplating building some retirement homes. We were weighing the pros and cons when he suddenly announced, "I think we need some more information."

Without saying another word, he got out the yellow pages, called one of the major insurance companies and asked to speak to one of their agents. Then, from a person he had never met or spoken to before, my friend proceeded to find out how many people live past the age of 55, what percentage reach 65, 75, what percentage is male, and female and a wealth of other valuable information. It took him less than five minutes and didn't cost a cent. I was impressed.

How did he do it? He operated from a principle that you would be very wise to learn: namely, that people are basically friendly and like to be helpful. It's that simple.

We think nothing of stopping a stranger and asking directions when we're lost. So why not in a business context as well? It's the same principle. Make it a game with yourself and have fun playing detective. See how quickly you can find the information you need.

John Gunn, a successful television producer, needed to get press accreditation fast for a film crew he was sending to Stonehenge in England. The normal channels weren't fast enough. "How to get it?" he pondered.

On a hunch he picked up the phone, called United Press International and asked to speak to the managing editor. He explained his situation. The editor wasn't exactly sure but gave him several phone numbers of people who might know. Two phone calls later, he had his information.

You too can use this principle. When you need information, just ask yourself, "Who would know?" Then get on the phone, introduce yourself and explain your situation and what it is you need. It's incredible what information you can get when you are willing to network with total strangers. And, by the way, don't forget to say "thank you".

Be Scrupulously Honest in All Your Dealings

BE FAIR AND HONEST in all your dealings. Even if doing so costs you money, in the long run it always pays. If you have the opportunity of short-changing someone without them knowing it—don't. Honour your word. Deliver what you promise. Keep your commitments.

There is no pride or inner satisfaction in lying or cheating, no matter what the reward. Short-term gain often leads to long-term shame and, in the final analysis, you must live with your decision.

I know I differ here from the "win at all cost" philosophy, but true success means more than an accumulation of dollars and cents. The dignity and honour that comes with honesty is an asset to oneself that's invaluable. Operate at the highest ethical and moral standards and people will respond to this, and respect you for it.

Good people regularly and consistently finish first, and don't let anyone tell you differently.

Not only do they finish first, but they have fuller, richer and happier lives.

Remember, we go this way but once. Enjoy the treasures and joys that life affords you, but most importantly, make the journey an honourable one. In the end, you'll be glad you did.

Remember Names

MOST PEOPLE don't remember names for the simple reason that they don't take the time and energy necessary to commit it to memory. They make excuses for themselves; they are too busy. Perhaps they are unaware that not remembering a person's name is sending a message to them, no matter how subtly, and it's not the type of message you want to send.

Conversely, every time you remember a person's name you are saying "You are important to me." Isn't that valuable?

Franklin D. Roosevelt knew that one of the simplest, most obvious ways of gaining goodwill was by remembering names and making people feel special. The stories are legendary about how the former president of the United States not only remembered the names of people he had met only once, but also those of their wives, and sometimes even their children as well. He took the time to do it because he felt it was important. Besides being a people-oriented president, he was a smart and savvy politician who knew all the tricks. In fact, he was the only U.S. president to serve three terms consecutively.

The ability to remember names is just as necessary in business and social settings as it is in politics, and its effect is just as powerful.

This being the case, it pays to take the time, before you begin each day's appointments, to imagine all the people you are likely to meet. Picture their faces. Then, match names to these faces.

Here's a valuable tip: if you have contact with clients or customers more than once, have their names written on a card filed with their title, and any other pertinent and valuable information. Add the names of their secretary and receptionist underneath—anybody with whom you have contact. Then, before you go back and see them, you can refer to it and have their names at your fingertips.

One top-performing executive I know who uses this system also likes to include their hobbies and likes and dislikes. Things like "son in little league," "wife likes antique furniture," "a Chicago Cubs fan." Then, when he's speaking to these clients after not seeing them for six months or more, he amazes them with this information. Does it impress them? What do you think?

This policy of remembering and honouring the names of friends and business associates was one of the secrets of Andrew Carnegie's stupendous success: it helped him to build a huge steel conglomerate at the turn of this century, and to amass a personal fortune of more than $400 million. At the time, he was the richest man in America. Remembering names was a skill to which he devoted valuable time and energy. He knew and understood the power available to those who master this simple courtesy, and he used it extensively and lavishly.

"We should all be aware of the magic contained in a name," said another Carnegie, Dale (no relation to above), in his classic book *How to Win Friends and Influence People*. "Realize that this single item is wholly and completely owned by the person with whom we are dealing and nobody else. The name sets the individual apart; it makes him or her unique among all others. The information we are imparting or the request we are making takes on a special importance when we approach the situation with the name of the individual. From the waitress to the senior executive, the name will work magic as we deal with others."

Enthusiasm Makes the Difference

FOR THOSE OF YOU WHO ASPIRE to greatness, remember the immortal words of Emerson, "Nothing great was ever accomplished without enthusiasm."

The word enthusiasm stems from the Greek word *enthous* meaning "inspired", and that's exactly what happens when you are enthusiastic; you become inspired. Everything changes. Your whole being becomes charged in some inexplicable way and you do things with the confidence of one who cannot fail. Your eyes sparkle, your words are powerful, minor day-to-day difficulties and annoyances are swept away effortlessly, and you feel alive and transformed. What's more, people who come in contact with you feel it too. They are attracted and swayed by it. Enthusiasm is infectious and almost always magical in its ability to influence yourself and those around you.

So the big question is, "Why don't more people use it?" Maybe it's because most people are waiting to feel enthusiastic rather than taking the steps to create enthusiasm within themselves. They are living the philosophy, as Woody Allen joked, that "life is 80% just showing up". And that's unfortunate.

Enthusiasm is too important an asset to simply leave to chance. If you want it, you should actively create it—and luckily for us, this can be done. Anyone who consistently practises the following three lists, will have enthusiasm working for them in whatever they do.

List No. 1

List 10 reasons why it's good to be alive:

1...

2...

3...

4...

5...

6...

7...

8...

9...

10...

Too often we get overwhelmed with the day-to-day affairs of our life. Stop for a few minutes every day and think about all the pleasures and joys that life affords you.

List No. 2

List 10 reasons why it's advantageous for someone to have your product or service.

1 ....

2 ....

3 ....

4 ....

5 ....

6 ....

7 ....

8 ....

9 ....

10 ....

Why should they buy your product? If you don't know, who does?

List No. 3

List 10 reasons why it's important that you are successful in life.

1..

2..

3..

4..

5..

6..

7..

8..

9..

10..

Tie your success to a greater goal or mission. Be motivated to succeed. Remind yourself again and again why it's important to be successful. Remember, your success helps many people but your failure helps no one.

Study these lists everyday until you have them memorized. Practise saying them aloud. Believe them absolutely. (If there are some points on your list that you still can't believe after a week of repeating them to yourself, take them off the list and replace them with something else.) The purpose of this process is to imprint these points into your consciousness. Then, when you're talking to others the points will just naturally and effortlessly flow into your conversation. People will become convinced because you are convinced. People will believe what you are saying because you sincerely believe it yourself.

Become so excited about why people should have your product that you can't help but share it with them. Feel motivated by a mission to help people, to give them an opportunity of having your product or service. It will become almost as if you are cheating them if you don't.

With enthusiasm you can accomplish almost anything. You climb to heights you previously thought unattainable. Your work takes on a whole new meaning and, what's more, it becomes fun and stimulating.

"A Champion Has to Be Able to Take a Good Punch"—Muhammad Ali

MUHAMMAD ALI was a boyhood hero of mine. One time when he was in Toronto to fight George Chuvalo (the Canadian heavyweight), I and a few of my friends skipped school to watch him train in his gym. It was thrilling to watch Ali in action, working the heavy bag and boxing with his sparring partners.

Perhaps he could see the awe in our faces or maybe he just felt paternalistic, but he decided to pass on some words of wisdom to the admiring crowd. "A champion has got to be able to take a good punch," he admonished. "A lot of fighters can throw good punches but a champion has got to be able to take a good punch and then another good punch and still keep on going."

Then, with a flurry of punches accentuating his point, he added, "That's what makes a champion."

In your pursuit of success and wealth there will be hundreds, if not thousands, of setbacks, disappointments and difficulties. Some will be minor; almost inconsequential. Others will be major crises that necessitate drawing all the courage, insight and determination that you can possibly muster. During these times, always keep an overview of the situation. Remember, a heavyweight match is 15 rounds. If you lose a few rounds, or even get knocked down, it doesn't matter as long as you get up and eventually win.

The same in life. The ability to consistently rebound from setbacks and disappointments is the mark of a champion. If you develop this trait, you are sure to win the big stakes.

Making New Contacts

NYBODY WHO SPENDS even just 10% of their time making new contacts will never be short of business. Sometimes the most obvious principles are the least applied.

Let me share with you an experience of mine. Many years ago I co-founded an entertainment agency, booking groups and acts into lounges and clubs across the country. My partner and I found that everything worked fine as long as one of us spent at least one week a month on the road, making new contacts.

There was only one problem; neither one of us liked to go on the road. So we procrastinated, made up excuses to put off travelling, tried different methods and ignored the obvious fact that when we didn't do it, we were neglecting an important ingredient to the success of our business. Time and again we would build up the business only to watch it slide, because we were not going on the road regularly and consistently.

When we followed our system everything worked like clockwork. Yet, if we didn't go on the road, business would suffer and we'd wonder why.

Finally, we woke up to the ridiculous situation we were putting ourselves through and solved the problem by hiring someone to work full-time on the road. Business boomed.

Looking after business means making new contacts, not once in a while, but consistently, week in and week out, month after month, year after year. New business is the life-blood of any organization.

Make sure you are not just paying lip service to this idea. Have a system in place that regularly produces new clients and customers for you. Too often we get busy just looking after what's in front of us. Be busy 90% of your time but reserve 10% of your time to developing new business. Make this a business rule not to be broken.

When a company or individual spends at least 10% of their working time drumming up new business, they have a solid footing for growth. Anything less is tempting fate.

Impressions Count

P EOPLE JUDGE YOU by what they know and what they see. And if they don't know you, they judge you only by what they see. Can you blame them?

Always put your best foot forward and present yourself in the best possible way.

Your office, your business card, your clothes, your manner, your style—it all counts. And don't make that foolish mistake of thinking your product or service will, alone, sway the deal. Impressions count, like it or not, so start impressing.

Don't Panic, There's Plenty of Time Yet to Make Your Fortune

1	2	3	4	5	6
1	16	31	46	61	76
2	17	32	47	62	77
3	18	33	48	63	78
4	19	34	49	64	79
5	20	35	50	65	80
6	21	36	51	66	81
7	22	37	52	67	82
8	23	38	53	68	83
9	24	39	54	69	84
10	25	40	55	70	85
11	26	41	56	71	86
12	27	42	57	72	87
13	28	43	58	73	88
14	29	44	59	74	89
15	30	45	60	75	90

THE SIX COLUMNS ABOVE each represent 15 years in a 90-year-old's life. Many people live to this great age. My grandfather will shortly celebrate his 104th birthday and, if he continues to be healthy, we'll soon need eight columns and not just six to chart his life. So, let's assume we're going to live a nice, long, healthy life to age 90 and have a look at it.

Sometimes it's good to stop and put your life in perspective. Where are you on the chart? Half way down the third? End of the second? Beginning of the fourth? Circle your age and look at where you are on the chart. Get a feel for your whole life. Don't delude yourself and think your life is over when it's probably just beginning. I invented this chart many years ago to help me put my life in perspective during a very difficult period. It helped me immensely and I've shared it with many since. It's good to stop now and then and look at where we are in life.

Just for fun, let's chart some of the people who have made fortunes in the marketplace. Steve Jobs, co-founder of Apple Computer, made his first million in the second column. So did William Gates of Microsoft. In fact, he made his first billion in the second column. However, most people who acquire fortunes reach their success in the third or fourth columns.

Eugene McDermott's little electronics store, which eventually became Texas Instruments, made him his first million in the third column. Edwin Land spent years painstakingly trying to develop a self-polarizing film, much to the ridicule and disbelief of people who knew it couldn't be done. It could and the Polaroid Corporation, which he founded, made him a huge fortune. This happened in the fourth column.

Mary Kay, a housewife with no business training, who wanted to do something after her children had left home, founded Mary Kay Cosmetics, which now has hundreds of millions of dollars a year in sales. Her success didn't start until the fourth column as well.

Colonel Sanders of Kentucky Fried Chicken fame, didn't reap financial rewards until the fifth column.

So don't panic and think life is passing you by. Relax and follow your game plan. There's lots of time yet to make your fortune.

Plan Your Work, Work Your Plan

HOW MANY TIMES have you heard a coach of a professional sports team explain a loss to the media in this way: "We didn't follow our game plan?"

Well, why on earth would they not follow their game plan if that's what they intended to do? Because, it's easy to stray off course. In the excitement and pressure of each play unfolding, you make decisions on the spur of the moment, sometimes in a split second. You get so caught up in the action of what's happening in front of you that you forget the original game plan and react.

So too in business. Often it becomes a "fix up what's in front of me right now" affair. Phone calls, deadlines, changing priorities, unforeseen developments, emergencies, new opportunities, problems all have a way of side-tracking you from your original plan.

Knowing this, its important that you always have an overview of what you want to accomplish each week,

each month, each year, and that you plan your wo
work your plan to achieve it.

Sure, you'll still have the phone calls, deadlines and new
developments clamouring for your attention but, if you
follow this simple four-step plan, you'll find you can easily correct your course when you get side-tracked, and
move quickly and effectively towards your goals.

- Step 1: Make a list
- Step 2: Do it
- Step 3: Review your actions
- Step 4: Make another list

Step 1: Make a List

Write down what needs to be accomplished this week.
What phone calls, letters, actions will move you forward
in your goals. Who do you need to see? What do you
need to do? What new information could you obtain that
would help you? What can you do to create more oppor-
tunites? What would make this a productive, successful
work week? Design a weekly list that moves you aggre-
sively towards your goals.

Step 2: Do It

Whatever can be done immediately—do it! What else can
be done today? Do it! And, one by one, you begin accom-
plishing what's on your list. As the Russian mystic Gurdjieff
so wisely advised: "Don't think of results, just do." Let

action be your vehicle to success. Accomplish everything you put on your list. Let this be your top priority.

Now, you might find that new developments will happen during your week and you want to add to your list. That's fine, add them, but never—and I repeat—never under any circumstances delete items from your list (unless they have been accomplished). The only time for deletion of an unfinished task is at the end of the week, during your review time. This is an important rule to follow as it gets you into the habit of following your plan.

Step 3: Review Your Actions

This is a step that most people omit in their work plans and that's a critical error. Reviewing your week is just as important as planning your week. In fact you should spend twice as much time reviewing your week as you do planning it because this is how you find out what's really happening with your work. Plans and good intentions are useless unless they are followed by action. Reviewing will reveal much to you.

In reviewing you need to ask yourself lots of questions:

- What got accomplished?
- What didn't? Why?
- What new developments occurred?
- What did I learn?
- What needs to be done next?
- What am I not doing enough of? Why?
- How can I be more effective?

Analyse and review last week's actions thoroughly before you plan your next week's activity. Remember, reviewing in many ways is even more important than planning. Take your time and find out what happened, what didn't and why before you move ahead.

Step 4: Make Another List

From the analysis and insights you obtained from Step 3, put together a new list for the upcoming week that moves you forward in your goals.

When these four steps are followed regularly, two important things happen. First, lots of work gets accomplished and this is important. Second, and this is equally important, you'll uncover patterns of behaviour in yourself that you never knew existed. In reviewing your list week after week, you'll discover how you consistently avoid certain types of tasks. This is a revealing and sobering realization. However, knowing this will assist you greatly in making the internal changes necessary to becoming more effective.

Four steps followed regularly every week. Sound simple? It's so simple that almost nobody does it. Oh, sure, people get inspired for a week or two, but I'm talking about a week-after-week, month-after-month reviewing system that allows you to get things done. Not once in a while but regularly and consistently. A steady, consistent method for achieving your goals.

Remember that knowing what to do and actually doing it are two totally different steps. This chapter tells you what to do. There's nothing radically new here and you probably know much of it. If you do, that's good. But that's just the first step. The little step. But can you, or will you, take the second, more important, step: that of actually doing it? That's the real question. And you can't answer this with your words alone or good intentions. Only your actions, over an extended period of time, will supply the crucial answer.

Persistence

I HAVE OFTEN THOUGHT that there should be a business hall of fame. A place where the application of great business principles could be enshrined along with the names of men and women who had mastered them successfully, so that we could all admire their victories and achievements. If there was, the following story would surely be included under the principle of "persistence".

Jerry Perenchio was an enterprising entertainment agent who correctly recognized that promoting the first Ali–Frazer title match could mean enormous profits for the shrewd promoter.

A little history is necessary at this point.

Muhammad Ali was stripped of his heavyweight title because of his opposition to the Vietnam war. Undefeated at the time, he was refused a licence to fight for three-and-a-half years. During that time, there were run-offs to decide a new champion. Joe Frazer, a brilliant young fighter, won it all and successfully defended his championship a number of times while Ali fought his battles in the law courts. Finally, Ali was allowed to fight again.

Two heavyweight champions both claiming the crown. Both rightful heirs. Both undefeated. It was a promoter's dream and Jerry Perenchio lay awake at night thinking about it: How he would market it to the public, to the networks, and sell foreign rights. He knew he could do it. There was a fortune to be made. However, there was one small problem ... he needed $10 million to pull it off. Where do you get that type of money? He made a list of 100 individuals who could bank-roll the project and began approaching them one by one.

Now, it isn't always that easy to get to see powerful and influential people. They are usually well-guarded by associates and secretaries, but the power of persistence paid off and he got to see the first man on the list. It was a very short interview and the man said "no". The second person he approached said "no". The third person said "no". The 20th person said "no". The 25th person said "no". How discouraging. How many times would the thought to give up cross your mind under these circumstances? Not once did it cross Jerry Perenchio's mind. He was determined to promote the fight.

The 26th person he approached was Jack Kent Cooke, the owner of the Los Angeles Kings and Lakers. Sitting in Mr. Cooke's office he presented his plan with the same enthusiasm with which he first conceived his idea. He spoke of the potential for making huge profits, how he could carry out his plan, how everyone would reap the rewards if a $10 million line of credit was put in his hands.

Jack Kent Cooke listened attentively to the young man standing before him. He studied Perenchio's face as the promoter quoted figures and projections and he made his decision. The answer was "yes".

The rest is history. The Ali–Frazer match was billed the fight of the century, and through the marketing wizardry of Jerry Perenchio, which was later copied by future promoters, it was the most profitable fight of all time. Everyone made their millions—Ali, Frazer, Jerry Perenchio and Jack Kent Cooke. The public was rewarded with perhaps the greatest fight ever seen and Ali lost one of his few professional fights.

A few months after the event, a journalist asked Jerry Perenchio what he would have done if Jack Kent Cooke hadn't put up the money. The young promoter replied without hesitation, "I would have gone to number 27."

Harnessing Your Subconscious Mind

FEW PEOPLE know how to use the powers of the subconscious mind to anywhere near its potential. That's unfortunate—this powerful, "hidden" mind, when properly directed, can guide you to anything you desire. It will supply you with all the ideas, plans and methods by which you may successfully achieve your goals, and bring to you the people, circumstances and events that you need to achieve this.

Mozart received his inspiration from within. Socrates was guided by his inner voice. Einstein spoke eloquently and often about the creative power of his subconscious. Thomas Edison, Marconi, Henry Ford, Madame Curie, the list of great men and women who attributed their success directly to this wonderful faculty goes on and on.

Conrad Hilton also learned this secret early in his life and it made him rich. Conrad made his fortune opening hotels throughout the world. His name is now synonymous with first-class accommodation. Conrad was a very savvy businessman with a strong desire to succeed—-but he had something more which gave him an advantage over his competitors. His associates referred to it as "Connie's hunches" and learned to respect them whenever they occurred. He knew well the knowledge contained within his subconscious and would go to it often for guidance and direction; he prospered in a way most people only dream of.

Our subconscious mind is different from anything we've ever encountered before. It appears to have access to infinite sources of knowledge and power. It transcends our normal limits and understanding of what is possible. And as incredible as it seems it can be directed to bring to us the things we most desire and dream about.

Sound astounding? Read on and learn the methods by which you too can access this power.

The Three Steps For Reaching the Subconscious

Step 1: Spend several minutes every day thinking about the fact that you have within you a second hidden mind. Your first and most important task is to re-educate your ordinary conscious mind to the existence of this other mind. Remind yourself how powerful and all encompassing it is. Allow yourself to be become inspired and excited, thinking how the subconscious can and will bring to you the plans, people and circumstances you require. That this is true will become apparent soon enough as you follow this process, but first you must get to believe that it is something real within you, something you can reach and influence.

This can only be accomplished by continually reminding yourself of its existence. Gradually, the realization that you possess something unique and dynamic within you will come to you. Until this happens, you will not be able to use it effectively. I cannot stress this point enough. You must walk before you run.

Step 2: Silently repeat to yourself each night before you go to sleep, and every morning upon rising, what it is you require from your subconscious. When you do this, play a little mental trick, and act as if you already have that which you are requesting. Boldly claim that the answers or events you desire are already yours, and feel as if they are. Immerse yourself in this feeling for several minutes. To help you understand what you're doing, take note of the interesting change of tenses contained in the following biblical scripture "Whatsoever things ye pray for and ask for, believing that ye have received them ye will receive them."

Notice it says you have to believe that you have received it before you will get it. If this sounds strange, remember, the laws of the inner world are different to what we normally understand. Take heed of the secret it reveals. You might recall that in a previous chapter I stated that your mind will come to believe whatever you repeatedly tell it. Any thought, belief or idea that is regularly repeated with feeling and emotion, will make an imprint upon your subconscious mind. Once this happens, nature will endeavour in hundreds of different ways to manifest this reality for you. Every morning and every evening, imprint into your mind the thought that you already have that which you desire.

98

Step 3: Spend several minutes attempting to feel the presence of your subconscious. Feel its closeness, its power even if you have to pretend in the beginning. The more real it becomes to you, the better you can use it. Treat it as a friend, a guide, a partner. Praise it. Acknowledge it. Resolve within yourself to let nothing stop you from making contact.

If you find yourself getting excited while reading this chapter, that is good, but I should warn you that, if you want to develop the ability of reaching your subconscious, you must be prepared to put in the necessary time and effort. Don't expect instant, spectacular results the first few times you attempt to tap into it. Only a steady, regular going within will give you the results you require. Your subconscious mind is wired in such a way that you have access to incredible powers. We've been wired this way for a reason. Learn how to influence this second hidden mind, and everything else in your life will look after itself.

Quality

QUALITY is not only desirable, it is necessary in today's business environment," says Du Pont Chairman and CEO E. S. Woodward, Jr. "Today's customer expects quality. He knows what he wants and what's more, he will look for it until he finds it."

A commitment to quality always pays handsome dividends to those who cultivate it. In today's highly competitive market, it is very clear that organizations and individuals not focused on quality are surpassed by those who are.

"The difference between the best and worst companies is measured in miles," a business consultant recently revealed to me. "But the difference between the best companies and the good companies is measured in only inches."

"Quality control" is a term that is bandied about in the business community but which is too often paid only lip service and then quickly forgotten. No wonder. To begin with, nobody understands what it means—it's too nebulous and abstract. Quality what? Why, the name itself is a misnomer. You don't control quality, you create it. Let's take the mystery out of quality control once and for all, and simply call it "a commitment to continuous improvement." Gino Giocandi, vice president of quality and production for Chrysler Motors, puts it in another way: "Quality is not simply a product attribute, it's a mind set."

AT&T chairman and CEO Bob Allen learned the importance of quality the hard way while he was playing end for his school's football team: "We were playing the number one, small college team in the country, and we were winning 13–7. One of the jobs I had on the team was filling holes on the football field before a game to be sure it was level. That day, I was rushed and went over the field rather quickly. Late in the game I had a chance to intercept a pass 20 yards from the goal line. I could see it. I could feel it. I could taste it. And, just as I reached out, I stepped in a hole I had missed earlier that day, and tripped. We lost the game 14–13, and to this day, I think about that incident when I think about quality. If I had done the job right, I'd have intercepted the pass and we would have won the game." It was a valuable lesson to learn, and he was lucky to experience first-hand the result of his negligence. Too often we don't even see the business we lose by taking short cuts and compromising.

Develop quality in everything you do. Quality thoughts, quality plans, quality products, all this combined together is what produces the winning formula. And as you strive for quality, never forget that it is an ever-moving target. It's like the four-minute mile: what was once terrific, even record-breaking, is now only second or third best.

Leisure

OFTEN WHEN I SPEAK to corporations I startle the audience by suggesting that the key to their success is often in working less, not more.

Leisure is just as necessary to success as work. It is the right balance of the two that allows you to perform effectively and consistently. Never forget that.

The biggest error in today's work habits, as I see it, is not that people aren't working hard enough (they surely are) but that they are not giving themselves enough quality leisure time, and their work is suffering as a result.

Leisure is not a reward for a job well done, leisure is part of the job. This is an important distinction. You don't oil and grease your car at the end of a long trip: you use the oil and grease all through the trip so your car will run smoothly.

Leisure allows you to relax, to let go, to give the mind a break, to turn off. This is necessary, for it is when the mind is in a state of relaxation, away from the quotas and deadlines, that creative, new ideas are given the opportunity to surface and make themselves known.

Universities have, for centuries, operated with this principle. They call it a sabbatical. Once, every seven years a professor is encouraged to take a year off to study or travel and, most importantly, to escape from the duties of professorship. The theory is that, after the year, the professor will come back invigorated, with new, stimulating ideas that in turn will enrich the university and its students. The theory is well-grounded in fact.

Now we can't all take a year's leave from our occupations, so we must be diligent in taking holidays, weekends and the occasional day off here and there. It is negligent, and foolish to do otherwise.

We have all seen and experienced the burn-out that happens with too much work in both ourselves and others. As the Zen saying goes "the bow kept forever taut, will break". This is a fact that we ignore at our own peril. Give yourself quality leisure time to relax and enjoy yourself not because you're lazy, but because you love success.

Here's a fact that might startle you although it is obvious for almost anyone to see: Most people are so busy working hard that they will never be successful. We have been taught, wrongly, that hard work is the way to success. Hard work without the balance of leisure almost always leads to failure. It is the leisure time between work that allows you to return to your project again and again, refreshed, with renewed vigour and enthusiasm.

It might be of interest to note that most major achievers in this world have reported that they made their biggest breakthroughs after taking time out for contemplation and reassessment. This is not hard to understand because when you are idle, your subconscious mind (the creative mind) advances full-steam ahead. It's very often during these idle times that brilliant, new ideas come forth.

Remember, it is the balance of work and leisure that will most surely and directly take you to success. Take time out this evening and list for yourself ten ways that you can include more leisure in your week. What do you enjoy doing? What gives you pleasure? Discipline yourself to include this in your daily routine.

And for those of you who foolishly think you can't afford the luxury to take leisure time, I've got a message for you: You can't afford not to. If you want to do quality work consistently, day in and day out, you have to give yourself quality leisure. Anything else is fooling yourself. And it's your work that will suffer as a result.

First You Work for Money, then Money Works for You

YOU INVEST MONEY for one purpose and one purpose only—to make more money. And that's what it does, in the most remarkable ways.

Most people think you need a lot of money to invest. But that isn't true. You can start with as little as a few thousand dollars. Let me show you how starting with just $2000 can put you well on the way to making your fortune.

The Law of 15%

The law of 15% guarantees that your money doubles in 4.9 years and that it's worth five times its value in 10 years. Now, some investments will return less than 15%, especially in the first few years when you do not have much to invest. But over a long period, with a varied portfolio, the smart investor can reasonably expect a 15% return on his money. So let's look at what you can do with a few thousand dollars. If you put $2000 into investments every year, at the end of 20 years you will have at your disposal over $200,000. Not bad for just $2000 a year.

But here's an even more attractive scenario. Begin with $2000 your first year of investing, then top it up with an extra $500 each year. So, the first year you invest $2000, the second year $2500 and so on. Now, if you are practising the principles of money and success, it shouldn't be too difficult to increase your investment portfolio by $500 over the previous year.

Then, after 20 years, here's what you do. Call your travel agent and purchase first class, around-the-world tickets for you and your family. Book yourself into the finest, most expensive hotels for your three-month, dream come-true holiday. Give yourself lots (and I mean lots) of spending money. Be lavish, extravagant - reward yourself in style for your successful investment strategy. Fifty thousand dollars should more than cover all this and with money to spare. Go ahead, you can afford it.

Then, upon returning home after your spectacular holiday, you will have more than half-a-million dollars waiting in your investment fund, earning you an impressive $75,000 in interest every single year for the rest of your life. In fact, it will have earned you almost $20,000 while you were on vacation. That's money making money for you.

And all this started with just a $2000 investment. Incredible? Hard to believe? Get out your calculator and check it for yourself. Why don't more people do it, you ask? I've got a secret for you. The smart ones are, and that's how they become financially independent.

What to Do When Someone Doublecrosses You

NOTHING. That's right. Absolutely nothing. Just forget it, you can't afford to let it sidetrack you.

The law of averages says that you're going to be cheated sometimes. Retail stores lose about 3% of their revenue yearly from shoplifters. Store-owners treat this loss as a part of doing business. They take precautions and prosecute when they can, but they still lose 3%. The important thing is, however, they don't carry around emotional baggage from every single incident. It's taken in stride.

How many times have you seen people completely destroy themselves with thoughts of hate and revenge? Have you ever seen hate and revenge work positively for someone? Why would you ever want it in you?

Sometimes it can be someone who is very close to you who cheats you, and that's hard. Sometimes it is someone you hardly know. In this world, not everyone operates with honesty and the highest integrity. This is unfortunate but a fact.

I know it's hard to do when you are the one who gets cheated but, believe me, the best and shrewdest move is just to forget it and move on. The sooner you do, the sooner you can be back on the track, with no heavy baggage to slow you down. Remember, your success and happiness count on it.

Five People Skills You Should Memorize

Fact 1: Business is a people-dealing-with-people activity and not a mechanical act.

Fact 2: People like to be appreciated, recognized and acknowledged.

Fact 3: A positive, optimistic person attracts people. A negative, complaining person repels people.

Fact 4: Every contact you have with a person makes an impression either favourable or unfavourable.

Fact 5: The greater your people skills, the greater your ability to achieve success.

Learn to See the Other Person's Point of View

I F THERE IS ANY ONE SECRET OF SUCCESS," said Henry Ford, "it lies in the ability to get the other person's point of view and see things from that person's angle as well as from your own."

Too often in life we're charging full-steam ahead, focused solely on what we want. We give little thought to what others want or need around us. It becomes our goals, our ambitions, our life, almost as if we're wearing blinders on our eyes. In a social context this is referred to as being selfish or self-centred, and is not an admirable quality. In business, it's simply foolish and short-sighted. For how can you effectively reach someone unless you fully extend yourself to that person and understand them? Putting yourself in their position and understanding their wants and needs gives you a perspective of the situation you could never obtain unless you took this effort.

A friend of mine, who is one of the most effective persuaders I know and a wealthy businessman, shared with me his secret for getting people to do what he wants. We were fishing aboard his private yacht and he was baiting his hook when he said to me, "John, you know how much I love pasta." And it was true. Whenever he talked about his trips to Europe, he inevitably ended up talking about the fabulous Italian cuisine. "I love pasta," he went on, "but I know that fish don't like it. They like worms. Now I hate worms. I would never eat one. The thought is revolting to me but if the fish want them, that's what I bait the hook with. I'm not stupid enough to give them what I want - I give them what they want."

I thought about what he had said throughout the fishing trip, and I have heeded his advice ever since.

Greg Singer runs a successful wholesale food company. He told me a story about how, one time, the buyer of one of his biggest customers balked at a price increase in one of Greg's products. "I knew that this buyer was under pressure to cut costs," he shared with me, "but on that particular product, our profit was negligible and we were long overdue for a price increase, so I refused to budge. I held my position and I was right to do so. But what I didn't do is see the overall situation of what he needed and wanted. I got stuck on a point of principle. Instead of giving in and maybe even losing a little on that product, I held my ground with my arguments and logic on why I had to raise the price. He reluctantly agreed.

A few months later I lost the whole account and I'm sure it stemmed from that incident. Now, I always put myself in the customer's position and look closely at the whole situation before I say or do anything. I don't ever want to lose another account by being short-sighted."

There is an old Indian saying, which goes like this: "Don't judge a man till you walk a day in his mocassins." Few of us realize that the traditional North American Indians, centuries before the white man ever stepped on their shores, operated with the highest moral and ethical codes. The old, traditional values are not seen in the Hollywood, cowboy-and-Indian movies. And when they said, "Walk a day in his mocassins," they meant to spend a full day where you would become that man. You would experience his thoughts, his fears, his worries, his needs, and his hopes. As he walked through the meadows and over the hill, you would suffer with him, worry with him and dream his dreams with him. You would not only see his perspective, you would become him and know his situation as intimately as he himself did. Then, and only then, with all this insight and knowledge could you adequately judge him.

As the saying goes, "There are two sides to every story. Two sides to every situation," and if you're operating from only yours, you're missing half of the picture. What's more, you're missing the most important half—that of the person you're trying to reach and influence.

The broader your scope and vision, the more effective you are in relating and dealing with people. And, when you come right down to it, relating and dealing with people is what business is all about.

Be a Good Listener

LISTENING *isn't* hearing. Hearing is the mechanical act of letting the other person speak. You can hear the words being said, but that doesn't mean you are necessarily taking it in. Listening is deeper than hearing. It makes an impression on you. It gives you information. Listening isn't a passive act, it's active. It's one of the most active, and productive talents you can develop.

When people speak of conversational skills, they usually mean being interesting, amusing or entertaining. What most people don't realize is that half the skills we need to develop as good conversationalists are listening skills. Does this surprise you? If it does, you're probably missing one of the most important ways of relating to others.

Let me introduce you to a super listener, and a super salesman, Joe Gandolfo. Joe sold more life insurance than any other person in the world. Forget a million dollars a year—one year, Joe sold a billion dollar's worth. Yes, that's one BILLION. With those credentials, he deserves to be heard. "Salespeople's biggest problem is that they do too much talking and not enough listening." He says "I believe that a good rule for a salesperson to follow is to count to five after the prospect has finished speaking before you say anything. This way you are sure there's nothing more he wants to say. That's important."

When your client or customer is speaking, they are sharing with you what they want, what they don't want, how they feel—giving you their perspective. Isn't that valuable? Too often, all this is missed in the rush to make the sale. Sometimes, your position and presentation are prepared even before you walk in the door. And, when your customer speaks, you are only watching for openings to jump in and get your selling points across, rather than carefully listening to what he or she is saying. And that's the problem. We think we already know what they're going to say. We think we know what they want.

Take a lesson from McDonnell Douglas, one of the world's top airplane manufacturers, who learned this principle the hard way. "We did not always listen to what the customers had to say before telling them what they wanted," admitted chairman and CEO John F. McDonnell.

All that changed quickly when they noticed their market share slipping drastically. Now, engineers and company representatives regularly work with their clients on their own turf, learning all they can about their customers needs. "We do a lot of listening now," says McDonnell.

One of the smartest and most successful businessmen I know hardly ever says anything. Whenever I'm in his company, I'm always amazed to find out that I'm doing most of the talking. Sometimes it's embarrassing. I asked him about it. "I like to let other people do the talking," he said. "It's amazing what information people will reveal to you, if you let them. You learn so much by listening."

We walk around as if we're receptive, but really we're so filled with our own opinions, judgements, knowledge and know-how that often nothing new can enter. When you really listen, you create a space within yourself to learn and accept and discover from others. It's so rewarding. What's more, people will experience you listening to them. They will appreciate it and respond accordingly.

Let me share a story with you. It happened to a colleague of mine after we spent a very lively evening discussing the principle of listening and how we often don't really hear what people are saying to us. The next morning, we were to get together again for an early meeting. He got up at 5.30 a.m. and was eating breakfast, when his young daughter came to join him. His wife was still asleep. After a minute or so, his little girl looked up at him and said, "Daddy, I love you." He was momentarily taken aback, and overcome with emotion, he asked her, "Why did you say that?" "Daddy!" she replied, "I say that to you every morning."

"I never knew that, or had really heard it before," he shared with me. We both just sat there and looked at one another in stunned silence.

Don't Let People Forget You

OUT OF SIGHT, OUT OF MIND" goes the old saying and there's a certain amount of truth in it. This being so, it is smart business strategy to stay in touch with as large a circle of contacts as possible. "But I don't have the time, I'm so busy," people lament. All I can say to that is, if you truly want to be successful, you make the time.

I'm going to introduce you to two individuals who have their own particular methods for staying in touch that work like magic for them. Take what you can from each of these methods, adding or deleting according to your own requirements and design your own system for staying in contact.

The Two-Minute Phone Call

Caryl Carter works as a salesman for a hardware wholesaler. It's a competitive business with lots of competitors vying for the retailers attention. But Daryl has discovered a unique system that works well for him. He calls it his two-minute phone call. Every working day between 9.30 a.m. and 10.30 a.m. he "works the phone" as he lovingly refers to it, making contact with as many people as possible.

"I never sell during this period," he says "If peole want to buy or talk longer, I tell them I'll call them back at 11, or 2, or whatever. I have my daily calendar in front of me at all times and I'm making notes about everything that's said. All I want to do is make contact and let them know I'm thinking about them."

I was intrigued by his method so I asked if I could watch him work one morning. He agreed. The next week on the appointed day I met him at his office and he had me sit at a desk opposite his with an extension phone so I could hear the conversations. It was quite revealing. Every call began the same, with him identifying himself and stating he had only a couple of minutes to spare.

Sometimes he asked questions: "Did you get this order?"; "Is everything okay?" "Anything more I can do for you?" Sometimes he informed them of upcoming events: "We've got some really good, new products coming up. I'll let you know about them next month." Other times, he just chatted: "How's the kids?"; "How's your baseball team doing?"; "Have you finished your basement?"; "How did your Rotary meeting go?" Sometimes he introduced him-self to new businesses. "I know you're happy with the outfit you're dealing with now but I'm just calling to say I'd love to have your business and we will look after you well if you ever decide to change."

Actually some of his calls lasted three to four minutes. Some less than a minute. But, on average, it was two minutes for each call and, sure enough, personal. Every call was concise and to the point. Nobody complained. Nobody was offended that it was a short call. And almost every one of them (28 out of 30 to be exact) said "Thanks for calling." They appreciated the contact. "People are busy," says Daryl. "They're happy that you respect their time. They just like to know that you're interested and concerned about them."

And he does this every working day. That's 150 personal contacts a week. And the next week another 150; 600 calls a month. Month after month after month.

Daryl Carter sells more than four times the next best salesman in the company. Any ideas why?

The Cards Never Stop

Joe Girard is called the world's greatest salesman. He's even listed in the *Guinness Book of World Records* for his selling feats. The guy's amazing. He sold more cars in his 15-year period at a Chevrolet dealership than any person alive. He would sell more cars in his average day than most good salesmen would sell in a week. On some days he would sell more cars than any other salesman would in a month.

How does he do it? He's perfected a number of selling skills which he uses with great dexterity. Joe's got great people skills. But, you can't sell anything until you have a customer in front of you and that's where Joe shines. He knows that word of mouth is the best way to build a business, so he designed a letter-writing program to make sure his customers would never forget him. Each month, every one of his customers would receive a card from Joe. "January was Happy New Year from Joe Girard, February was Happy Valentine, March was Happy St Patricks' Day," and so on, straight through to Thanksgiving and Christmas.

"They loved those cards," said Joe, with a big grin on his face. "Twelve times a year my name appeared in my customers' homes in a very pleasant way. Towards the end of my career, I was sending out 14,000 cards a month. I was spending more on stamps than the average car saleman makes in a year." Was it worth it? You bet. Over his career Joe sold more than six cars a day in an industry where the average is one or two a week.

Somebody once said, "When you buy a car from Joe Girard, you have to leave the country to get away from the guy." Joe took it as a compliment. It was.

The Transformation

You transform your life by choosing wisely your thoughts.
You transform your life by changing your beliefs.
You transform your life by empowering your relationships.
You transform your life by strengthening your self-image.
You transform your life by adopting good habits.
You transform your life by learning new skills.
You transform your life by increasing your actions.
You transform your life by transforming yourself.
It can't happen any other way.
Begin now!
The time is ripe.

Self-Image

WHILE ALMOST EVERYONE would agree on the importance of a good, healthy self-image few people know how to acquire one or understand how they formed the one they now possess.

Our self-image is exactly what it says: an image made up of ideas about ourselves that we have formed over the years. Once this image becomes imprinted on the subconscious mind and forms a structured pattern, it takes on a life of its own and we forget that it is something we have created, which can be changed and altered to better fit our present needs and requirements.

Let us look closer at how self-image is formed. In childhood, when our "worth" was first established, we accepted all kinds of ideas about ourselves. If our parents were loving and supportive, we most likely felt relatively good about ourselves; if our parents abused, ridiculed or belittled us, we may have a less positive self-image.

As we grew up and moved away from our parents, out into the world of our peers and other adults, countless other experiences impressed themselves on us.

Building a strong self-image

A car that is not maintained properly will inevitably become a wreck. A house that is not kept will become rundown and dilapidated. Your self-image, likewise, must be maintained if you want it to be strong and vibrant. It is through ignorance and neglect that a self-image deteriorates. Take responsibilty. Take care of your self-image as you would take care of yourself.

Life is full of temporary disappointments, heartaches, failures and problems, and if we are not careful these can easily drag us down. We need to regularly reinforce our self-image in order to keep it healthy. We can do this by setting up a regular program to feed our mind with positive, uplifting, inspiring thoughts about ourselves. We can even cheat a little and include thoughts that aren't yet true. Remember, your subconscious mind will accept any thought about yourself that you regularly think, and that idea will eventually become part of your self-image.

You will become whatever you consistently think about yourself.

- Timid thoughts create a timid person.
- Confident thoughts create a confident person.
- Weak thoughts create a weak person.
- Strong thoughts create a strong person.
- Thoughts with purpose create a person with purpose.
- Visionary thoughts create a visionary person.
- Thoughts of helplessness create a helpless person.
- Enthusiastic thoughts create an enthusiastic person.

- Loving thoughts create a loving person.
- Successful thoughts create a successful person.

YOU are responsible for your own self image and YOU are responsible for creating and maintaining it.

Self-Confidence

Insist on self-confidence. Settle for nothing less than a firm belief and conviction that you can, and will, succeed. If you have had an unfortunate childhood, put it behind you; you are here now and your future awaits. If you have failed previously, so what? The only thing that counts is what you now think and what you do with these thoughts. As your self-image becomes stronger and more confident, life's situations will become easier, for as you change, so does everything around you. It is entirely in your hands.

Creating and Maintaining a "Success Vibration"

NOTHING SUCCEEDS LIKE SUCCESS. It's an old saying but a true one. Success creates an aura and an energy in and around a person that somehow naturally and effortlessly attracts more success. It has momentum and power to it that can be used again and again to great advantage. Those that understand this make it a habit to create and maintain a "success vibration" for themselves.

To create a success vibration, start thinking successful. You do this by regularly focusing on all the positive qualities you possess. Take time out right now to make a list of at least ten positive qualities about yourself. Search for things to acknowledge. Don't just acknowledge the obvious, acknowledge everything. Include such things as "I'm good at my job. I dress well, I'm a positive person. I'm creative." Don't feel silly or think it doesn't matter. Your positive qualities are just as real as the negative ones. Too often we put too much emphasis on the negative part of us. Let's get out the trumpet and celebrate our good points.

When you have your list, let your mind linger for several minutes on the success you already are. Go ahead and feel proud. Feel great. Feel successful. Do this regularly every day and you'll start to build a success vibration.

Let every success you've ever achieved, both past and present, be a potential source of power to you. Often, when we accomplish something, we feel good about it for a few days, or if we're lucky, a few weeks, but then we move on to other matters. All too quickly we leave behind the feelings of accomplishment; soon we forget that we have even achieved them. We let go and lose the success vibration that was created from our achievement. This is a complete waste of powerful "success energy." We can re-use success energies from past achievements again and again, with very positive results, but, unfortunately, we have never been taught how.

Focus regularly on all your achievements, even something that happened five or ten years ago can be used. But that's the past, you might say. True, it is the past, but the success energy produced by focusing on it happens here in the present, and can assist you to further successes. So don't dismiss it.

Learn to pat yourself on the back often. Look for anything that makes you feel strong, victorious, successful, and good about yourself. Acknowledge anything and everything, and use it to create a vibration of success.

Make a list of 12 reasons why you think you'll succeed at your goal. If you can think of a dozen reasons why you will succeed, you'll never be intimidated by temporary setbacks or by what other people tell you. Refer to it whenever you're feeling depressed or defeated. It will be like a safety net that catches you when you fall. Let this list inspire you back again to your success vibration.

Success comes to those who become success-oriented, who have a success vibration. Failure comes to those who allow themselves to become failure conscious. We all have successes and failures. We all have victories and defeats. Allow the failures and defeats to fade in memory—to go their way. Forget them. Let them go. But your successes and victories should never be forgotten. They should be held on to and relived forever. Wear them within yourself like a victory banner and let them empower you. It will serve you well.

Have Fun Three Times a Day

HAVE FUN three times every day. Sound too frivolous? Not taking your work seriously? Not at all. The mind needs diversification and thrives on variety. When you can mix fun and business together and make it a daily habit, your work is more effective.

How much time does it take to have fun? Sometimes, just a few moments. You can have fun in almost any situation. When you are driving to work and enjoying a good song on the radio—that's fun. A joke shared with a fellow employee, a chapter read in a good novel, even a brisk walk in the sunshine or a workout at the gym can be fun if you are enjoying it.

We must ensure that everyday has some fun in it. Make a list of all the activities that can be fun and see how many of them you can include in your daily routine. Remind yourself you're having fun. Sometimes we get so busy in our minds, we don't even realize what's happening. Don't miss out on your fun while you're having it.

Fun gives you energy. It empowers you, refreshes you, helps you work better. So don't deny yourself these benefits.

Make fun an important part of every single day. It is smart, healthy, empowering, nourishing, productive, beneficial and, oh yes, I almost forgot the most important part … it's fun.

Let Great Men and Women Shape Your Life!

HERO WORSHIP shouldn't disappear with adolescence. At least not if we're smart. It can and should be a life-long source of inspiration and motivation for us.

Many of the most famous and influential people we know have had their mentors and heroes to which they aspired.

John Lennon idolized many of the old rhythm and blues greats long before he ever became a Beatle. He had their pictures on his wall and he used them as inspiration when he first began playing guitar.

Woody Allen watched the Marx Brothers' films hundreds of times and dreamed of being as funny and talented. It's no secret that Groucho Marx was a major influence on the talented filmmaker.

Ted Turner studied the Greek classics in university. His father, a very practical businessman, couldn't understand why his son was wasting his time with the classics. "What possible use will it be to you?" he exasperatedly demanded of his son one day.

What he didn't realize is that Ted was conditioning his mind with images of the fabled Greek heroes who seized opportunities, turned sure defeats into victories and surmounted countless obstacles to win. Sound familiar? It certainly does to those who have watched the meteoric rise and breathtakingly daredevil moves by one of America's most exciting businessmen.

A millionaire clothing manufacturer shared with me how, in her early struggling years, she would draw inspiration from other successful women. She had pictures on her wall of prominent women who had made it. They became her mentors. Every time she looked at the pictures it gave her encouragement. If they could do it, she could too, she reminded herself. And she did.

There is an ancient fable about a famous archer named Swift. He received his name because his arrows were always the swiftest in flight and deadly accurate. From fair to fair he travelled, and no one could match his skill. He was honoured and revered everywhere he went and, as the years went by, became very famous and wealthy.

One day, a gangly, awkward teenager, who was showing great promise as an archer himself, pushed through the crowd to see his idol. Mustering all the courage he had, he meekly asked the great archer if he would teach him how to be as great. Swift laughed and laughed as he looked down at the skinny, awkward young man who stood before him and said, "You think you can be as good as me?" Swift continued to laugh as he brushed past him, ignoring his request. The crowd was laughing too and the young man felt humiliated and shamed. However, he noticed that Swift had dropped one of his arrows as he left, and quickly scooped it up with no one seeing.

Undeterred by his idol's rebuttal, the young man went into the woods, perfecting his skill there for five years. Each day, before practising, he would go to a small altar he had constructed, worship the arrow that Swift had dropped and imagine that his idol was there teaching him. This ritual took on such meaning that he actually began to believe Swift was there in spirit, guiding and directing him.

Soon, word spread that there was a new, brilliant archer who lived in the woods. Perhaps he was even better than Swift, the gossips said.

Swift, hearing this, became enraged and sent out emissaries to find this so-called great archer and challenged him to prove himself at a tournament between the two of them.

Word spread quickly and thousands gathered on the day they set aside to challenge one another. Swift shot with his usual brilliance, with each arrow hitting the bull's eye. But the young man was even better (sometimes his arrows split right through the one's Swift had shot) and he was awarded the prize. "Who taught you how to shoot like that?" a crestfallen Swift asked in disbelief. "Why, you did, master," came the humble reply. And indeed, in a way he had.

Napolean Hill, author of the classic *Think and Grow Rich,* and financial mentor to some of the most prominent men in his day, shares how he uses great men from the past to assist him. He would create imaginary meetings with Abraham Lincoln, Thomas Jefferson, Andrew Carnegie and Henry Ford—men whom he admired and respected. And, in these meetings, he would discuss various business problems with them. Much to his amazement, these great men would advise him on how to best proceed. He credits much of his success to this system.

Did these men really advise him? Of course not, but the inspiration aroused by his imagination allowed high quality ideas and solutions to flow into his mind.

All big companies that pride themselves on excellence have what is called their "war stories". IBM, 3M and Hewlett Packard have them; stories of past employees who performed great feats under difficult circumstances. People who achieved spectacular results. Men and women who did the impossible; who surmounted all odds and won. They become part of the companies' lore, like folk legends and inspire others to carry on in the same tradition.

We all need to know that what we're trying to accomplish can in fact be done. Perhaps it will take an almost super-human effort, but if we harness all our resources and determination, we have to believe that it can be done. That it's not impossible.

When we model ourselves after those who have achieved greatness, take on their character, their strengths, their determination, we in turn become like them and better ourselves in the process. It is said that during the Cuban Missile Crisis, President John F. Kennedy read and re-read the bigraphies of Winston Churchill and other great men. A man of courage himself, he nonetheless drew from the well of inspiration in his time of crisis.

Do you have role models? Heroes? Mentors? If not, you're missing out.

Be Someone Who Makes a Difference

HOW DO YOU make a difference? Ironically, you can do it through almost every action and word. You do it when you wipe your child's face, when you cheer up someone who's depressed, when you visit your parents or grandparents, when you congratulate someone on a job well done. One doesn't have to change the world to make a difference, just become more aware and caring.

Fay Stockill makes a difference. She has a self-help programme which she takes into the prisons, teaching the inmates self-esteem and positive thinking. "The one thing these people have a lot of," she says, "is time to think." She also realizes that the thoughts they think in prison will undoubtedly determine what happens to them when they're outside again. So she helps. It's a nourishing, enriching, well-thought-out programme created by a woman who cares—and the results are spectacular. Several times I've gone to the prisons with Fay and watched her work. Fay is a small, somewhat shy woman. The last person you'd expect to be doing this type of work, but she believes passionately in what she is doing. When she talks about the human potential, her eyes light up. The prisoners love her, and the respect is etched on their faces everytime she enters the room.

To hear these grown men, some hardened, some bitter, share their most intimate experiences—to see them open up and sometimes cry, is humbling. All the while, there is Fay supporting them, encouraging them, feeding them with positive messages, making them believe in themselves because she believes in them. You would think she would be welcomed with open arms by the prison authorities. She's not. She fights the bureaucracy every inch of the way. First she's being paid, then, after a few months, there is no more money in the budget. It's disheartening, but Fay takes it in stride. She continues in spite of all this because she believes she can make a difference.

Anna Aviles is a music teacher at public school 161 in Brooklyn, New York. Her students are mostly underprivileged kids who don't always believe in themselves. Who can blame them? Their surroundings give them little cause for hope. But she believes in them, and her goal is to make them feel good about themselves. "If they can feel good about themselves in even one area of their life, then they can feel good about themselves in other areas, too," she states with conviction. "All they need to do is succeed in one area ... just one, and that triggers their belief that they can do it in others as well."

So they mount plays together. Ten-year-olds, twelve-year-olds, fourteen-year-olds, rehearsing and staging Broadway hits. And when they finish, it becomes a local community

135

event. They begin at 7.30 a.m., one hour before school starts, and they stay after school as well. They learn co-operation, discipline, how to begin and finish a project, how to turn an idea into reality, and they have fun too. And when it's all over, they leave with a feeling of accomplishment and a belief in themselves. They know they have succeeded in this one area of their life, and they begin to dream of the future with a different perspective. Maybe, just maybe, they think, they could do it again. Ann Aviles is making a difference.

Glyn Evans is a partner in Stonehenge Filmworks, a television and film video production house in Toronto, Canada. I met him when they did some promotional work for us several years ago. Glyn belongs to the Big Brothers Association, an international organization helping boys who don't have fathers. Once a week, he takes his little brother on an outing—to a baseball game, a movie, or just spending some time with him. They've developed quite a bond. Glyn works long hours. Often he's so busy, he doesn't really have the time to go on these outings, but he makes the time. I've seen him leave early from an important meeting to keep an appointment with his little brother. It's a commitment he's made, and he keeps it. Glyn Evans is making a difference.

Several years ago, our company decided to devote 10% of our profits to a Making a Difference fund, which we created. The money would then be dispersed to groups, individuals and organizations who are making a difference, who are helping to make this world a better place. It's funny, it seemed so revolutionary and radical at the time. Little did I realize what joy, pleasure and satisfaction this decision would bring. We decided right in the beginning to focus on smaller, grass-roots organizations that don't get much attention and who really needed our money.

This past year we've thrown parties for underprivileged children, sponsored Fay Stockill in her prison work, helped an unemployment drop-in center, paid the rent for a women's shelter, and given grants to disabled athletes, Greenpeace, youth groups and many others. It's the most wonderful feeling you could ever imagine and I feel in a small way we are making a difference. We all have to start somewhere. Yet, it's only the beginning.

Recently, I was watching television; the head of a major multinational company was defending its corporate record to a probing reporter. "We're good corporate citizens," he shot back at the suggestion they might not be doing enough. And it got me thinking—"good corporate citizen," what does that mean? Paying taxes? Grants to charities? Support for the arts? Or is there more? What are the responsibilities of corporations and individuals for that matter? Can and should we do more for our communities and the world we live in? Anita Roddick has some strong views on this.

Anita is the founder of The Body Shop International. Her story is already a legend in the United Kingdom. A 33-year-old housewife, with two young daughters, had an idea for a store that would feature natural lotions and potions for the body. With a $7000 bank loan, she and her husband proceeded to start up shop. Now it operates successfully in 37 countries and is projected to be a $1-billion company by 1995. But it's not their growth that is so unusual—it's their attitude. The Body Shop is almost as well known for its passionate environmentalism as for its cosmetics. Roddick has incorporated her environmental beliefs into the business—offering only biodegradable products, for example, and providing refillable containers. The company even has an Environmental Projects department. And it uses its shops as the base for a series of highly visible campaigns to save the whales and stop the destruction of rain forests, among many other worthy causes.

She believes that businesses should do more than make money, create decent jobs and sell good products. "Companies should actually help solve our major social problems—not just by contributing a percentage of their profits to charities, but by using their resources to come up with real answers. Business is just another form of human enterprise, so why should we expect and accept less from it than we do from ourselves?" she argues convincingly. And Anita has a vision: "I believe quite passionately that there is a better way. I think we can rewrite the book on business. I believe you can trade ethically, be committed to social causes and empower your employees all at the same time."

I believe the time will come when corporations will recognize they have a responsibility to make a difference in the world; that they will be inspired by the challenge and embrace it at first slowly, then eagerly; that the time will come when profit will be only one of the measures of success. An important one to be sure but where community responsibility and global solutions will be high on their priority list as well.

It will take people, in responsible positions both in government and business, to make courageous decisions and commitments. It will take more people like Fay Stockill, Ann Aviles and Glyn Evans who, despite their busy lives, take the time to make a difference. It will take a change in priorities and values and beliefs in all of us. But, it's not impossible. It can happen if we really want it.

I have purposely taken a positive perspective in all this for a good reason. I believe the image we hold of the future plays a role in helping that future emerge. The potential strength of our society will be created by the intensity and energy of our images of the future. The future is not fixed. It doesn't just happen. The choice of whether or not we move in this direction rests very much with us. It's our decisions and actions that will ultimately make the difference.

Social activist, and former secretary of health and education in the U.S., John Gardner said, "People want to work hard on something they believe in. People are basically good and loving and caring but what's happening is that most of us don't know where to start." How can I, as a single individual, make a difference, we seem to be saying. The answer is simply by starting with the fragment of the universe that is right in front of you.

A woman friend of mine shared with me how, when she goes to the beach, she always makes sure she takes away not only her own litter, but a little extra as well. "I don't make a big issue of it," she says. "I don't try and clean the beach. But everytime I go, I take at least one extra piece of garbage back with me, something I didn't bring. That way I feel the beach is better off for me having been there." That's beautiful. And we can adopt that sentiment into all aspects of our lives. We can make a difference.

139

Don't Forget the View

ABOUT SIX YEARS AGO, when I was doing a seminar in Sydney, Australia, one of my course participants asked me to see his father. His father had recently gone to the doctor and discovered he had cancer in more than 60% of his body, and there was no possibility of recovering. He was told he had only three months to live. The family was devastated; his father was overcome with shock. This all happened within a few days.

I agreed and a time was set up for me to see him. I took a taxi to his house, and he greeted me at the door. He thanked me for coming. The family had arranged that we be alone for an hour. It is an hour I will never forget.

We talked, for 15 or 20 minutes, about life, and its impermanence. He then invited me outside to his back yard: it had a stunning view of the water and the Sydney Opera House, and you could see sailboats throughout the harbour. It was magnificent. And then he said something that shook me to the core. He said, "John, I'm a very practical man with practical ideals. I believe in working hard to support my family and give them a good lifestyle. I guess you could say I'm a workaholic ... or was a workaholic," he corrected himself with a thin smile. "I've lived in this house for 20 years. It will be 20 years this September. Four days ago, when I returned from the doctor's office with the news that I had only three months to live, I was crushed. I came out here and sat where we're sitting right now and looked at the view. Looked at how beautiful and serene it was. And I suddenly realized I had never seen the view before. Not really. Oh, sure, I had come out here and looked at it hundreds of times but I was always thinking of my business. There was always something on my mind. I never really just stopped to enjoy it. And it's so beautiful ..." his voice trailed off and he began to cry. We both just stood there. Two grown men sharing the anguish of the moment.

I wish I could say this story had a happy ending, but it didn't. The father died a few months after I saw him. However, there is a lesson here to be learned. Simply: "Don't forget the view." And the view is what happens to you each and every day of your life. The view is your life. Don't miss it. Don't let it pass you by. John Lennon said it beautifully: "Life is what happens while we're busy making other plans." And that's what happens. We get busy.

We continue to live our lives focused on future destinations: when the mortgage is paid; when my obligations are fulfilled; when I'm rich; when I meet that special someone; when things are different. Yes, that's fine, but what about today? What about this very moment?

There is a Zen practice called "drinking deeply" that involves breaking through the restrictions of a busy mind to fully appreciate everything for what it is. So when you're eating, you experience eating fully: the taste, the colour, the texture of the food. When you're in the garden, everything becomes special: the flowers, the sky, the air, the hum of the insects,· the feel of the earth on your feet. Nothing else is needed. Everything just is. And you are there, noticing and appreciating. It takes practise but we too can learn to do this in our own way.

Sometimes one needs to turn everything upside down to make sense of it. What if feeling the wind on your face, hugging your child, laughing with a friend, taking the family out on a picnic, helping someone in need, watching the sunset, carrying out the garbage, going for walks...what if this is what it's all about? What if this is what's really important? It's something to stop and consider as we race through our lives.

Andy Warhol said that life is art, and he was right. Every person's life is a piece of art. And the greatest masterpiece one can ever create is that of a life well lived.

Have fun, be successful, make lots of money, be someone who makes a difference, and, above all else, don't forget the view.

Further Information

For information concerning courses, seminars, confer-
ences, and audio and video cassettes, enquire at:

Zoetic Inc.
PO Box 38648
121 East 1st Street
North Vancouver
British Colombia V7L 4T7
Canada

Mind Power
PO Box Q379
Queen Victoria Building
Sydney NSW 2000
Australia

Mind Power
PO Box 27211
Mt Roskill
Auckland 4
New Zealand